THE

	Defini-tory Hypo-theses 1	ψ 2	Nota-tion 3	Atten-tion 4	Inquiry 5	Action 6	. . . n.
A β-elements	A1	A2				A6	
B α-elements	B1	B2	B3	B4	B5	B6	. . . Bn
C Dream Thoughts Dreams, Myths	C1	C2	C3	C4	C5	C6	. . . Cn
D Pre-conception	D1	D2	D3	D4	D5	D6	. . . Dn
E Conception	E1	E2	E3	E4	E5	E6	. . . En
F Concept	F1	F2	F3	F4	F5	F6	. . . Fn
G Scientific Deductive System		G2					
H Algebraic Calculus							

TRANSFORMATIONS

BY

W. R. BION,

D.S.O., B.A., M.R.C.S., L.R.C.P.

MARESFIELD LIBRARY
LONDON

First published in 1965 by
William Heinemann Medical Books Ltd.
Reprinted 1984 with permission
of Francesca Bion by
H. Karnac (Books) Ltd.
58 Gloucester Road,
London S.W.7.,
England

Second Impression 1991

Printed & bound in Great Britain by
BPCC Wheatons Ltd, Exeter
ISBN 0 946439 07 9

ACKNOWLEDGMENTS

AGAIN it is a pleasure to me to acknowledge help and criticism of this book from a number of colleagues and friends who have read it in proof.

Professor Elliott Jaques, Miss Betty Joseph, Mr. Money-Kyrle and Dr. H. Segal have all helped with advice and criticism. I am also indebted to Dr. J. O. Wisdom for many helpful criticisms of my previous work, and in particular of *Learning from Experience*, which have made me more aware of the pitfalls in this one. But whether I have avoided them is another matter. I would thank them all, but would not have them debited with my faults.

As always there remains my debt to my wife which I can acknowledge but cannot repay.

W. R. B.

INTRODUCTION

I had hoped to write this book so that it could be read independently of *Learning from Experience* and *Elements of Psycho-Analysis*, but I soon found this impossible without an intolerable degree of repetition.

The other two books are therefore still necessary for the understanding of this one. I regret this; there are some things I said before which I would now say differently. But any reader who thinks the subject is as important as I do will find it rewarding if he can think the thought through despite defects of presentation.

W. R. B.

CHAPTER ONE

SUPPOSE a painter sees a path through a field sown with poppies and paints it: at one end of the chain of events is the field of poppies, at the other a canvas with pigment disposed on its surface. We can recognize that the latter represents the former, so I shall suppose that despite the differences between a field of poppies and a piece of canvas, despite the transformation that the artist has effected in what he saw to make it take the form of a picture, *something* has remained unaltered and on this *something* recognition depends. The elements that go to make up the unaltered aspect of the transformation I shall call invariants.

The artist is not the only person involved in looking at a picture; recognition of what the picture represents could not occur if the observer were to rely exclusively on his sense of smell. The wider his experience of art the more likely he would be to interpret the painting correctly.

In many pictures the effectiveness of the representation would depend on perspective. A peculiar feature of this domain is that a completely circular pond, for example, might be represented by an ellipse, or a path with borders running parallel to each other might be represented by two lines that meet. Indeed the representation of pond or path would be less adequate if it were a circle or parallel lines. Accordingly we assume that in ellipse and intersecting lines, circular pond and parallel borders, is some quality that is invariant under artistic creation.

Suppose now that we view a stretch of railway line that is straight as far as the eye can see. The two lines of the track will be seen to converge. We know that if we were to test the convergence by walking up the line this convergence would not be confirmed; but, if we were to walk far enough and to look back the way we had come, the convergence would appear to lie behind us and to be confirmed by our sense of sight; the two parallel lines meet in a point. Where then is this point?

One theory would explain the apparent meeting as an optical illusion. I propose not to accept this explanation, for in a domain in which the sense of sight only is employed correlations based on common sense[1] are not available; furthermore, the explanation, though valid in its sphere, does not promote development in the domain of this investigation.

In Euclidean geometry definitions of terms such as "point", "straight line" and "circle" are so closely wedded to marks on paper and similar realizations that these definitions, which are really suggestive descriptions, serve well enough. But points and straight lines as defined in Euclidean geometry are not things-in-themselves. The mathematician has found that the extensions which his subject demands are not served by these definitions. The point and straight line have to be described by the totality of *relationships* which these objects have to other objects.[2] I shall leave on one side the problem of the extent to which the totality of relationships can be either explored or ignored.[3] The mathematician can investigate invariants common to circular object and ellipse, that represents it, by algebraic projective geometry. In his investigations statements about length, angles or congruence cannot find a place in the theorems of projective geometry, though they are a part of Euclidean geometry; therefore psycho-analysts need not be dismayed if it can be shown that there is no place in their theories for measurement and other entities that are a commonplace of disciplines accepted as scientific. Just as there are geometrical properties invariant under projection, and others that are not, so there are properties that are invariant under psycho-analysis and others that are not. The task is to find what are the invariants under psycho-analysis and what the nature of their relationship to one another.

What is the relationship of the point at which parallel

---

[1] See Bion, W. R.: *Learning from Experience*, in which I discuss the use of the term "common sense".

[2] The definitions of such commonplace physical substances as zinc are summaries of relationships, described as "properties".

[3] Heisenberg, W.: *Physics and Philosophy*, p. 82.

lines meet to the points at which lines that are not parallel meet? The railway lines of my example can be seen to meet; the surveyor would not confirm the finding and nor would the neurologist. Though this problem is not of consequence to the psycho-analyst it may resemble problems which are. To them I shall now turn.

In his paper, "Fragment of an Analysis of a Case of Hysteria" (1905),[1] Freud gives a description of a patient Dora. The paper may be regarded as analogous to, but differing from, a painting, in that it is a verbal representation of an analysis; we can gain an impression of the experience as we can gain an impression of a field of poppies though the original field of poppies or the original analysis are unknown to us. There must then be something in the verbal description of the analysis that is invariant. Before the invariants in the printed description can be effective certain precedent conditions must exist; the layman must be literate: the invariants in Freud's description I shall accordingly describe as "invariant under literacy."

Not all laymen would understand the same thing from the printed description; "invariance under literacy" therefore is not an adequate limitation. We must therefore consider briefly some of the problems that are involved in establishing the limitations of the field. We are introduced to some of these problems in Freud's Prefatory Remarks to this paper; he points out that it can be read as a *roman à clef* designed for private delectation. The understanding of such a reader will depend on invariants under prurience and is not what Freud intends to bestow on his reader. He indicates this by his reference to the *Studies in Hysteria* and subsequent developments of psycho-analytic technique; invariants under pornographic literature[2] are not invariants under psycho-analysis. To use the visual arts to provide an analogy, invariants in photography are not the same as invariants in impressionist painting.

For my purpose it is convenient to regard psycho-analysis

[1] Freud, S.: "Fragment of an Analysis of a Case of Hysteria" (1905), Standard Edition, Vol. VII.
[2] See Freud, S.: Prefatory Remarks to "Fragment of an Analysis. . . ."

as belonging to the group of transformations. The original experience, the realization, in the instance of the painter the subject that he paints, and in the instance of the psycho-analyst the experience of analysing his patient, are *transformed* by painting in the one and analysis in the other into a painting and a psycho-analytic description respectively. The psycho-analytic interpretation given in the course of an analysis can be seen to belong to this same group of transformations. An interpretation is a transformation; to display the invariants, an experience, felt and described in one way, is described in another.

Freud's reference to developments that had taken place in psycho-analytic technique indicates one direction in which this inquiry must be pursued. Since psycho-analysis will continue to develop we cannot speak of·invariants under psycho-analysis as if psycho-analysis were a static condition. In practice it is undesirable to discard established theories because they seem to be inadequate to particular contingencies; such a procedure would exacerbate a tendency to the facile elaboration of *ad hoc* theories at times when it were better to adhere to established discipline. It is therefore advisable to preserve a conservative attitude to widely-accepted theories even when it has become clear that some adjustment needs to be made. For my present purpose it is helpful to regard psycho-analytical theories as belonging to the category of groups of transformations, a technique analogous to that of a painter, by which the facts of an analytic experience (the realization) are transformed into an interpretation (the representation). Any interpretation belongs to the class of statements embodying invariants under one particular psycho-analytic theory; thus an interpretation could be comprehensible because of its embodiment of "invariants under the theory of the Oedipus situation."

The advantage of classifying psycho-analytic theories as members of groups of transformations will be discussed later,[1] but I shall anticipate some of the main considerations here. The painter by virtue of his artistic capacity is able to

[1] See Chapter 2.

transform a landscape (the realization) into a painting (the representation). He does so by virtue of invariants that make his representation comprehensible. The invariants depend on the technique he employs: thus the invariants in an impressionist painting are not the invariants of a painting by a member of, say, a realist school of painting. Similarly, the invariants in a description of a family situation by a layman will not be the same as they are in a description of the same family situation by a psycho-analyst using oedipal theory. The various psycho-analytic theories enable the psycho-analyst to effect similar transformations. Analytic theories, or groups of theories, can be combined to transform the realization into a representation or series of related representations (interpretations). The analytic theories thus associated may then be classified by their association with the type of transformation (and its associated invariants). The type of transformation will depend on the analyst and his assessment of the demands of the clinical situation. Thus an analyst may employ theories of splitting and the oedipal theory to effect a transformation such that the invariants ensure understanding in his patient. His theories, transformation (or group of theories) and interpretation (or group of interpretations) will be analogous to the artist's techniques, transformation and end-product. Just as impressionism can be regarded as a method of transforming landscape into a painting, so the grouped analytic techniques are part of transformation of analytic experiences into interpretation. As the painter's transformations vary according to the understanding his painting is to convey, so the analyst's transformation will vary according to the understanding he wishes to convey. Kleinian transformation, associated with certain Kleinian theories, would have different invariants from the invariants in a classical Freudian[1] transformation. Since the invariants would be different so the meaning conveyed would be different even if the material transformed (the analytic experience or realization) could be conceived

---

[1] In practice I should deplore the use of terms such as "Kleinian transformation", or "Freudian transformation". They are used here only to simplify exposition.

of as being the same in both instances. Similarly the painting
of the same scene by a realist and an impressionist would
convey different meanings. Further particularization is
achieved, for one Kleinian analyst's transformation and
therefore interpretation would differ from another's. Nor
would the interpretations by two impressionist painters be
alike though both painters could be recognized as belonging
to the same school (of transformation). For the problems of
diagnosis the approach I am making may have value in that
clinical entities might be defined and classified according to
the transformation[1] (I refer now to the method and its
component theories) and invariants employed.

Throughout this book I suggest a method of critical
approach to psycho-analytic practice and not new psycho-
analytical theories. By analogy with the artist and the
mathematician I propose that the work of the psycho-analyst
should be regarded as transformation of a realization (the
actual psycho-analytic experience) into an interpretation or
series of interpretations. Two concepts have been introduced, transformation and invariance. The book will be
devoted to these concepts and their application to the
problems of psycho-analytical practice. I use borrowed
philosophical and other terms for psycho-analytical purposes
because the meaning with which they are already invested
comes near to the meaning I seek to convey. When I
write "transformation" or "invariance" I leave it to be
understood that I am discussing psycho-analysis. What I
mean by these terms will, I hope, become clearer as I use
them.

Psychotic mechanisms appear in the course of a psycho-
analytically controlled breakdown, but the analyst may be
called upon to deal with them after such a breakdown has
occurred, or, because something has happened, despite the
work of the analyst, to precipitate such a breakdown during
analysis. I discuss the latter contingency because the
material illuminates transformation and invariance as a
function of patient and analyst. The clinical description is
designed for reasons of discretion to be impossible to apply

[1] Transformation is discussed in detail later. See Chapter 2.

to any one of whom I have heard, but the reader will not be misled if he treats it as true.

The man[1] could be regarded, in view of the predominance of psychotic mechanisms and bizarre behaviour, as a borderline psychotic. Analysis seems to proceed slowly and there may be little evidence open to observers or members of the family that his behaviour is different from what it has been. Then a change: friends or relations who have been denying that there is anything the matter cannot ignore his illness. He has been strange: he spends hours seated morosely in a chair; he appears to be hearing voices and seeing things. On this latter point there is some doubt; in the consulting room it is difficult to say if the patient is describing a delusion or indulging his fancy. In analysis he is hostile and confused. There is sudden deterioration. The alarm of relatives is evident in letters and other communications from them or the family doctor. There appears to be reason for the analyst to be alarmed, or, if he is not, to lay himself open to grave miscalculation and consequent blame.

In such a situation the common view is so pervasive that it is difficult to suppose that the analyst's anxieties and those of the relatives could be regarded profitably as anything other than rational and appropriate to the facts. Preservation of an analytic view, of what is taking place, is made difficult because it can fit so easily into a pattern of denial, by the analyst, of the seriousness of his predicament. In such a situation the analyst will take such steps as his experience in the management of analytic cases dictates. He will try to assess the contribution that his own psychopathology may be making. I mention these points without discussion save for their bearing on transformation and invariance. In the material I wish to include the analyst's anxieties and, in so far as he has access to them, those of the patient's relatives and friends. The analyst's main concern must be with the material of which he has direct evidence, namely, the emotional experience of the analytic sessions themselves. It is in his approach to this that the concepts of transformation and invariance can play an illuminating role.

Change from an analytical experience, confined to the

[1] Later referred to as A.

consulting room, to a crisis that involves more people than the pair is remarkable for a number of features. It is catastrophic in the restricted sense of an event producing a subversion of the order or system of things; it is catastrophic in the sense that it is accompanied by feelings of disaster in the participants; it is catastrophic in the sense that it is sudden and violent in an almost physical way. This last will depend on the degree to which analytical procedure has produced a *controlled* breakdown. Since, for the purposes of this description, it is easier to deal with phenomena whose characteristics are exaggerated I shall rely on the description of events pertaining to the less analytically controlled episode. It must be borne in mind, however, that the analytically controlled event is more difficult to deal with in that the reactions being more restrained the elements in the situation are correspondingly unobtrusive and difficult to detect. Furthermore, in the analytically controlled event the catastrophic elements bear the same relationships to other elements as katabolic features bear to anabolic features in metabolism. I shall therefore ignore complications which I do not for the present wish to introduce.

To return to my illustration: there are three features to which I wish to draw attention: subversion of the system, invariance, and violence. Analysis in the pre-catastrophic stage is to be distinguished from the post-catastrophic stage by the following superficial characteristics: it is unemotional, theoretical, and devoid of any marked outward change. Hypochondriachal symptoms are prominent. The material lends itself to interpretations based on Kleinian theories of projective identification and internal and external objects. Violence is confined to phenomena experienced by psychoanalytical insight: it is, as it were, *theoretical* violence. The patient talks as if his behaviour, outwardly amenable, was causing great destruction because of its violence. The analyst gives interpretations, when they appear to be appropriate to the material, drawing attention to the features that are supposed by the patient to be violent.

In the post-catastrophic stage, by contrast, the violence is patent, but the ideational counterpart, previously evident, appears to be lacking. Emotion is obvious and is aroused in the analyst. Hypochondriachal elements are less obtrusive. The emotional experience does not have to be conjectured because it is apparent.

In this situation the analyst must search the material for invariants to the pre- and post-catastrophic stages. These will be found in the domain represented by the theories of projective identification, internal and external objects. Restating this in terms of clinical material, he must see, and demonstrate, that certain apparently external emotionally-charged events are in fact the same events as those which appeared in the pre-catastrophic stage under the names, bestowed by the patient, of pains in the knee, legs, abdomen, ears, etc., and, by the analyst, of internal objects. In brief, what present themselves to the outward sense of analyst and patient as anxious relatives, impending law-suits, mental hospitals, certification, and other contingencies apparently appropriate to the change in circumstances, are really hypochondriachal pains and other evidences of internal objects in a guise appropriate to their new status as external objects. These then are the invariants or the objects in which invariance is to be detected. I shall turn now to the relationship of violence to the change that has taken place from pre- to post-catastrophic.

The change is violent change and the new phase is one in which violent feelings are violently expressed. By analogy with an explosion, the patient's state of violent emotion sets up reactions in the analyst and others related to the patient in such a way that they also tend to be dominated by their over-stimulated internal objects thus producing a wide externalization of internal objects.[1] In practice in the pre-catastrophic stage, the violence of the emotions has to be deduced and this is true even of the post-catastrophic stage if the breakdown is analytically controlled. Though adequate as a theory there is advantage in using an explosion and its expanding pressure-waves as a model. I shall do so.

The catastrophic event may be described in terms of the

---

[1] Contrast with this state—shock, the seeping away of sanity into his own "mental tissues."

theory of transformations: this involves regarding the transformation, implied by employing the theory of transformations, as itself belonging to the group of transformations.
That is to say that I transform the *facts* I describe by regarding them in a particular way. My description is therefore a
transformation, analogous to the artist's painting that is a
product of the particular artist's approach. For convenience
I shall call my approach here transformation 'A.' Within
this usage I have used the term "transformation" in three
ways that need to be distinguished from each other: the
term "transformation" related to (i) the total operation
which includes the act of transforming and the end product:
for this I shall use the sign T; (ii) the process of transformation: sign $T\alpha$; and (iii) the end product: sign $T\beta$.

Further distinctions are needed to minimize ambiguity.
In my illustration it is possible that we shall need to discuss
the lay point of view, such as that involved in concluding
that the patient is not simply a normal person being difficult,
but that he is mentally disturbed. Evidently the final
opinion $(T\beta)$ will not be the same when the facts are viewed
in the light of a belief that the patient is normal as it is when
the belief is that the patient is mentally disturbed. If
discussion of the lay point of view is necessary we shall need
to distinguish T still further; for example, by a sign T (lay)
or a sign T (lay: normal) or T (lay: mental). To illustrate
this notation: if we wish to categorize the description given
by relatives who think that the patient has gone mad, it is
first necessary to categorize the transformation (T). In this
instance it would be: T (lay: mental). This however by
itself could mean all of three things: (i) the relatives' point
of view, (ii) the particular processes of thought leading to
the description, and (iii) the description itself. Since we are
concerned only to employ a sign for the last of these, the
full sign would be: T (lay) β.

In general it may be said that the cultural background
against which analytic work must be done is hardly a matter
with which the individual analyst can concern himself; yet
the culture may concern him. In the exceptional case,
notably Freud himself, psycho-analytic work has profoundly

affected the social outlook. Therefore it is a matter of importance to analysts that the public image of our work is not distorted to produce a climate of opinion in which difficulties, already great, are enhanced. That image will be influenced by patients, their analysts, and the societies and groups that analysts form. In the event of catastrophic change such as I postulate in my illustration there is a further transformation T (public), and therefore, since we are concerned with the end product, the opinion the public has formed: T (public) β. In some instances it may be of consequence to determine the content or meaning of the realization represented by the signs T (public), T (public) α, and T (public) β.

In the catastrophic event the concern of the analyst must be with transformation manifested in the patient. In this notation the representative signs are T (patient) standing for change in his point of view and including T (patient) α, the processes by which he effects the change from the realization to T (patient) β; the end product or transformed material is what is presented to the analyst.

Finally, we come to the analyst. In general terms the analyst's point of view differs from those we have considered because it is psycho-analytic. He will observe the pre-catastrophic state and make his own description, usually embodied in interpretations. In so far as the catastrophe may affect the armoury of theories on which he relies there will be a need to represent two transformations, one pre-catastrophic and the other post-catastrophic. This change must be reflected in the sign employed for the transformation. If he makes no change the signs will be T (analyst) and this will include T (analyst) α and T (analyst) β. If there is a change we can replace "analyst" by a sign representing the cycle of transformation, pre- and post-catastrophic.

If the reader considers the first chapter in the light of his experience he will realize that any apparent strangeness lies in the method of approach and not in the experience described. It will help understanding if he will satisfy himself before he reads further that phenomena described are already familiar to him.

CHAPTER TWO

THE term "transformation" may mislead unless the limitations of the implication of "form" are recognized. In painting, in geometry, it is safe to think in terms of form, but I am concerned with a function of personality in the process of being represented and it may introduce errors to suppose that a function of personality has a form. In severely disturbed persons a transformation T (patient) may be a deformation. Such a patient, abandoning one transformation for another, may produce T_2 (patient) β which has no obvious resemblance to T_1 (patient) β. Suppose that T_2 (patient) β is a shapeless lump, the term "deformation" is not likely to mislead. But if T_2 (patient) α is the patient's experience of being greeted by the analyst and T_2 (patient) β is the patient's representation of the event as a hostile attack made on him by the doctor, it may seriously obstruct understanding of what has taken place in the mind of the patient to suppose that either T_2 or $T_2 \beta$ have, or are, forms.

The grid in *Elements of Psycho-Analysis*[1] affords a method of escape from the implications of "form" through resort to signs for abstract categories (the various grid compartments) to represent the content of $T_2 \alpha$ and $T_2 \beta$. A sign to represent the realization would denote, to take the example in Chapter 1, the landscape as a thing-in-itself, and therefore distinguish it from both $T_2 \alpha$ and $T_2 \beta$. The sign would denote something that is not a mental phenomenon and therefore, like Kant's thing-in-itself, can never be known. I introduce the idea of the thing-in-itself to make clear the status of $T_2 \alpha$ and $T_2 \beta$ as signs for mental phenomena.

The use of these signs may be clarified by an illustration: The patient enters and, following a convention established in the analysis, shakes hands. This is an external fact, what I have called a "realization". In so far as it is useful to regard it as a thing-in-itself and unknowable (in Kant's

[1] Bion, W. R.: *Elements of Psycho-Analysis.*

12

sense) it is denoted by the sign O. The phenomenon, corresponding to the external fact, as it exists in the mind of the patient, is represented by the sign T (patient) α. This sign I mean to replace by a grid category. The grid category is determined by picking on that category to which my clinical observation of the patient's behaviour seems most closely to approximate. Suppose the handshake is intended as a denial of hostility that the patient experienced in a dream about me. His action would then fall in a category in column 2 and row C. The sign then would be C2.

The associations following this start to the session would have yielded the evidence for choosing the sign C2. In addition I expect to find evidence on which to determine the category in which I shall place the representation that has resulted from his transformation, T, of the episode, O, (thing-in-itself), to T (patient) α and thence to T (patient) β —this last being the representation, his representation, of the episode. This sign T (patient) β I shall now replace, as I have already done with T (patient) α, by a grid category. Once more the grid category must be determined by assessment of the associations. Suppose the evidence suggests that the patient's experience is that my handshake was a sexual assault on him. The context shows me that this approximates to a definitory hypothesis; I expect accordingly to find the category in column 1. If, from my knowledge of him, I am convinced that the patient is not experiencing this as a thought or idea or even as a dream, but as an actual fact, I assess the category to lie in row A—the β-elements. The category with which I replace T (patient) β is A1.

Using the facts (of my illustration) to achieve a formulation in terms of a theory of transformations, I arrive at the following: the total analytical experience is being interpreted as belonging to the group of transformations, denoted by the sign T. The experience (thing-in-itself) I denote by sign O. The patient's impression, T (patient) α, is replaced by grid category C2. The patient's representation, a resultant of the transformation he has effected, T (patient) β, is replaced by grid category A1. Since we have not yet come to a decision about the nature of the process of transformation it is convenient to employ a sign showing that the abstraction represented by T is unsaturated.

The emotional experience of my illustration, as I have described it verbally, can be represented in the form of an equation as follows: $T = C_2 \rightarrow A_1$.

This formulation can be regarded as analogous to a model: a man observing that certain elements are constantly conjoined, binds the conjunction by using a sign, say the term "dog". Once the elements observed to be constantly conjoined are bound by the term "dog", the person thus binding them can set about discovering what meaning is to be attributed to the term "dog".[1] By analogy, we, having bound the constantly conjoined elements of the analytic experience by the formulation $T(\xi) = C_2 \rightarrow A_1$, may now resort to further analytical experience for evidence which will provide us with meaning: in other terms, to saturate the unsaturated element (ξ); or, again, to put it in another way, we hope to find evidence from analysis for a more precise understanding of this particular patient's transformation. The investigation of this and other analytical experiences should in time enable us to see different types of transformation and perhaps to arrive at some classification of the different sets of transformation which together make up the group of transformations.

In practice this means that if a patient is encountered with whom the analyst has experiences of which my illustration is typical, the analyst should be able to distinguish phenomena of the type $C_2 \rightarrow A_1$. This would enable him to formulate characteristics of T implying the existence of sets of T. It may help to clarify my meaning if I anticipate the findings of our investigation by provisional formulation of what such sets of transformation might be. Further it will serve the purpose of setting bounds to the area in which we search for clinically based theories of transformations. I therefore propose provisional hypotheses as an apparatus for

---

[1] An analogical counterpart can be seen in the group: if I succeed in binding a constant conjunction by writing this book the group can take over the task of discovering what it means.

further inquiry.[1] They are to be replaced by formulations to which the realization of psycho-analytic practice more closely approximates.

I assume that mental disorders fall into one of two categories, neuroses and psychoses, and ignoring existing criteria used to distinguish one category from the other I shall attempt to distinguish them on the basis of the theory of transformations. I shall therefore assume that the material provided by the analytic session is significant for its being the patient's view (representation) of certain facts which are the origin (O) of his reaction.

In practice this means that I shall regard only those aspects of the patient's behaviour which are significant as representing his view of O; I shall understand what he says or does as if it were an artist's painting. In the session the facts of his behaviour are like the facts of a painting and from them I must find the nature of his representation (or, in terms of my notation, the nature of that which I denote by the sign T (patient) β). From the analytic treatment as a whole I hope to discover from the invariants in this material what O is, what he *does* to transform O (that is to say, the nature of T (patient) α) and, consequently, the nature of T (patient). This last point is the *set* of transformations, in the group of transformations, to which his particular transformation (T (patient)) is to be assigned. As I am concerned with the *nature* (or, in other words, meaning) of these phenomena, my problem is to determine the relationship between three unknowns: T (patient), T (patient) α, and T (patient) β. Only in the last of these have I any *facts* on which to work.

I shall call on clinical experience to illustrate the next stage in this investigation. The patient[2], a man of 40, married, with one son, whose childhood was spent in a well-to-do professional family of father and mother with three older brothers, had complained of insomnia. The occasion was the last session before a weekend, and he commenced it by saying he had dreamt that a tiger and a bear

---

[1] In fact another instance of binding—this time by provisional hypotheses.
[2] Referred to earlier as A (see pp. 7 and 10).

were fighting. He felt dreadfully frightened lest the animals in their ferocious maulings would stumble across him and kill him. He woke in dread with a shout ringing in his ears. It was his own shout. The dream reminded him of a story by a famous big game shot; he could not remember the name of the man. The tiger who was very well known to be the fiercest of animals was driven off its kill by a bear. But the bear had its nose bitten off. It made him shudder to think of it. (Here he screwed up his face and shuddered.) He could not think of any more. He went on after a pause: The girl he was once engaged to for a year had broken off the engagement because she wanted to be free to flirt with other men. It still made his blood boil. Pepper was the man she married. He was very fond of pepper himself. Pepper was hot stuff with the girls. So unlike himself who was always afraid of them. With his wife it was different, but she was dull. At this point he became confused and I omit the rest of the session.

I have chosen this illustration because it lends itself easily to interpretation. The reader can see that the stimulus of the week-end break might be the trigger for the dream and its associations. There is no lack of analytic theories that might be appropriate and with the knowledge of the patient I had—he had been in analysis with me for two years—I was able to narrow choice of interpretations to two or three. But even two or three interpretations can be an embarrassment when one only is wanted and that one correct in the context in which it is given. I am therefore ignoring here, and throughout this book, any discussion of psycho-analytic theories. I am however concerned with theories of psycho-analytic observation, and the theory of transformations, the application of which I am here illustrating, is one of them. Can this theory be applied to bridge the gap between psycho-analytic preconceptions,[1] and the facts as they emerge in the session?

First I shall apply the theory to my own account of the

---

[1] The grid category of "psycho-analytic pre-conceptions" as I use the term here is F4, not D4 or 5, because I use the term "pre-conception" to denote "use" not "genesis".

session: something occurred during the session—the absolute facts of the session. What the absolute facts are cannot ever be known, and these I denote by the sign O. My description is of the facts as they appear *now* to have been at the time they took place: it is a description of phenomena and the description can be represented, in conformity with the theory of transformations, by the sign T (analyst) β. My mental processes, by which the phenomena were transformed to become the description I have given (T (analyst) β) are represented by the sign T (analyst) α. Since I may want to talk about them even if I do not know what they are, it is convenient to be able to refer to them by the sign T (analyst) α.

I shall not discuss T (analyst) α or T (analyst) β except to point out that the session is the stimulus for discussion and can therefore be represented by O and my description of it by T (analyst) β. As the patient is to be discussed we shall be concerned with a different O, call it O (patient), and T (patient) α and T (patient) β. To discuss O (patient) I shall represent the phenomena, to which he reacted by T (patient) α and T (patient) β, as T (patient).

The first question is, What is O (patient), or, to express it in more conversational terms, what was the patient talking *about*? One answer is that he was talking about the week-end break. Let us examine this.

Such a solution cannot be arrived at by any ordinary view of his statements. To re-state question and answer in terms of transformation theory: O (analyst), the patient's statements, have been transformed by me, my mental processes being represented by T (analyst) α, to form a view, T (analyst) β, from which I deduce that T (patient) = the week-end break. Or rather that I have assumed that a week-end break, O, exists, and that the phenomena associated with O by the patient is something I denote by T (patient). In some circumstances it may be adequate to say that the patient was talking about the week-end break. It may be adequate to say this in an analysis. But, as analysts know, such a statement will not provide an answer that is adequate to all breaks in analysis. The question itself lacks precision and is yet overloaded with meaning. In discarding the conversational expression for something more precise but less encumbered with meaning, for example, T (patient), and then falling back on the analytical experience and procedure to invest it with meaning, lies the justification for "naming". Analytically trained intuition makes it possible to say the patient is talking about the primal scene and from the development of associations to add shades of meaning to fill out understanding of what is taking place. I have chosen this session because, although the reader has not the emotional experience itself, he will be able to make deductions from the material that will serve for understanding this that I am saying without my own deductions. I shall proceed on the assumption that the reader will draw his own conclusions and from them see in what way his view of the session might be enhanced by a theory of transformations.

I shall now consider the state of mind in the patient which makes him see the week-end break as he does, that is, the *process* of transformation T (patient) α. By what mental processes does the patient come to experience the week-end break as an object of fear? What, when he contemplates the week-end break, does he see? In other words, what meaning are we to ascribe to T (patient) β? The material should show both what he sees and how he comes to see it as he does, the process of transformation and the product of that process.

I shall propound my views in general terms known to every analyst. As far as the process is concerned I assume that transference plays a predominant role and that the end-product, T (patient) β, is what an analyst would call a transference neurosis. The aspect of transference important in transformation is that which Freud[1] described as a tendency "to repeat as a current experience what is repressed" instead of recollecting it as a fragment of the past. He goes on to say, "This reproduction appearing with unwelcome fidelity always contains a fragment of the infantile

footnote[1] Freud, S.: *Beyond the Pleasure Principle* (1920). Standard Edition, Vol. 18, p. 18.

sex life, therefore of the Oedipus complex and its off-shoots, and is played regularly in the sphere of transference, i.e. the relationship to the physician." It is this "unwelcome fidelity" that helps to make the term "transference" so appropriate. At its worst the fidelity of the reproduction tends to betray the analyst into interpretations that have a repetitive quality seeming to suggest that what the patient says about someone else applies almost unchanged to what he thinks and feels about the analyst. Though such interpretations are a parody of what transference interpretations should be they contain a germ of truth. The feelings and ideas appropriate to infantile sexuality and the Oedipus complex and its off-shoots are *transferred*, with a wholeness and coherence that is characteristic, to the relationship with the analyst. This transformation involves little deformation: the term "transference", as Freud used it, implies a model of movement of feelings and ideas from one sphere of applicability to another. I propose therefore to describe this set of transformations as "rigid motions". The invariance of rigid motion must be contrasted with invariance peculiar to projective transformations.

In the clinical illustration I said the patient became confused; I shall use an instance of the type of confusion he displayed for an illustration of a session for this chapter, but it will be from a different patient[1] and will be more intense. Here it is: The patient came in, but, though he had been attending for years, seemed uncertain what to do. "Good morning, good morning, good morning. It must mean afternoon really. I don't expect anything can be expected today: this morning, I mean. This afternoon. It must be a joke of some kind. This girl left about her knickers. Well, what do you say to that? It's probably quite wrong, of course, but, well, I mean, what do *you* think?" He walked to the couch and lay down, bumping his shoulders down hard on the couch. "I'm slightly anxious . . . I think. The pain has come back in my knee. You'll probably say it was the girl. After all. This picture is probably not very good as I told him but I should not have

---

[1] Referred to later as B.

said anything about it. Mrs X. . . . thought I ought to go
to Durham to see about, but then" and so on. I cannot do
justice to the episode because I remember only the general
impression and the general impression depending on changes
of tone expressing depression, fear, anxiety, confidentiality,
and others, was itself intended to give a general impression.[1]
The short report is verbally nearly correct; yet as I read it
again I see it is a misleading record of the experience. I
shall therefore make another attempt to describe this fragment of session but without attempting verbal exactitude.
After his pause of uncertainty he whispered his good morn-
ings as if he were pre-occupied with an object he had lost
but expected to find close at hand. He corrected himself in
a tone that might imply a mental aberration that had led
him to think it "good morning". The speaker of the words
"good morning", I gathered, was not really the patient, but
someone whose manner he caricatured. Then came the
comment that nothing could be expected. That was clear
enough, but who was making the comment, or of whom
nothing could be expected, was obscure. It might have been
myself; I did not think it was he. Then he spoke of the joke.
The way this term was used implied that the joke had no
tincture of humour about it. To me it could mean a cruel
joke, but such an interpretation depended on an assumption
that the words retained the meaning that they would have
in sane conversation and that the emotion expressed, by and
with them, had the value that it would have in ordinary
speech. When he spoke of "this" girl it was evident that I
was supposed to know her; in fact I did not nor did I know
whether she had left her knickers lying about or given notice
on account of some episode connected with her knickers.
"What do you say to that?" meant that in either case I
would know as well as he did what her behaviour signified,
though, as his next sentence showed, the significance (un-
mentioned) attached to her behaviour by both of us was
probably mistaken, girls being what they are.

When he lay on the couch he did so as if trying to express
surreptitiously his wish to damage my property. I thought

[1] See Chapter 1.

his next comment compatible with this surmise in that it might mean that, being confused with me and yet detached from both of us, he hazarded a guess that I was anxious at his violence, that I supposed him to be anxious and not aggressive, that he thought the feelings he experienced were what I would call anxiety. His reference to the pain in his knee was typical of certain very rare statements in that it meant "The pain in my knee, which I now experience, is what you as analyst think is really the girl inside me." Such a statement meant that despite evidence to the contrary he had knowledge of my analytic theories and that he was now having an experience which I would explain by that particular theory. It might mean that he wished me to know what experiences he was having and that the correct interpretation could be arrived at through the theory of internal objects. Such interpretations were rare but previous experience had convinced me that they occurred and had the significance I have attributed to this one. But the flatness of tone, the tortuosity of the communication and the ambiguity made it probable that I would either fail to grasp the latent meaning, or, in searching for some such meaning, would fail to notice the almost obvious sense.

His "after all" is typical; it is meaningless, but can act as a stimulus to speculation. Subsequent remarks meant that what had been taking place in the session was a pictorial representation, an externalization of a visual image, not likely to be regarded by me as good and therefore evacuated by me with such force that this fragment of his personality would be projected as far away from me as Durham is from London.

It will be observed that this, my second account of the episode, contains a very high proportion of speculation. The speculations depend on my theoretical pre-conceptions. In addition to classical analytical theory I have had in mind Kleinian theories of splitting and projective identification. I expected to find that some part of the confusion would be illuminated by applying the theory of projective identification to the patient's inability to distinguish between himself and myself. I also assumed that experience of hallucinations, as I have described them in my paper, "On Hallucinations", would stand me in good stead. But beyond preserving an awareness of such a background of theory I allowed myself to be as open to clinical impressions as possible. I have already indicated what some of these impressions were. The experience, as usual, was one of stimulation and frustration. The sense of being at a loss, which will be apparent to the reader, is not quite so profound in the consulting room as the written account makes it appear, because the clinical experience affords a mass of detail that cannot be communicated in print; even though it is grasped imperfectly it is sure to make an impact. Yet an account that contains so much speculation to so little fact must be unsatisfactory to a scientist. To what extent is the patient's communication the most direct and informative instrument he can employ, obscure though it may appear? Is its obscurity due to the difficulty of the matter of the problem for which he seeks help or is it due to his need to conceal? The analyst's task is to distinguish one from the other. In terms of T, it is necessary to determine whether T (patient) β is characterized primarily by the need to conceal O or by the need to give as direct a representation of O as possible in view of its obscurity to him; in the illustration I have given the characteristic of T (patient) β is revelatory rather than obscuring.

It may seem perverse to judge it as revealing, especially since in fact the patient could, though extremely rarely and then only for short periods, speak coherently. My reason lies in the experience of many sessions of which the cumulative effect was to give an impression of O. The impression was often difficult to express in words. Sometimes it was strong, but hard for me to formulate without feeling my interpretation, even to myself, was fanciful. At other times I was satisfied that my formulation was a correct translation into words and that it was a valuable communication; such occasions made interpretations to the patient likely to be analytically sound. The decision that the communication is revelatory must depend on the strength of the impression received by the analyst and this weighed against the fact that the patient appears to choose an obscure method of communication. Later I shall consider the possibility of classifying the types of communication[1] T (patient) β, as well as the process of communication T (patient) α. In my next chapter I shall discuss the illustration in terms of the theory of transformation.

[1] See Chapter 5.

CHAPTER THREE

THE clinical illustration of Chapter 2 made a distinction between the patient's experience O and the analyst's experience O. When the stimulating experience is the analytic session itself, O is the same for patient and analyst and the distinction has to be made between the processes by which the patient transforms his experience to achieve his representation of it and the processes by which the analyst does so; similarly between the patient's representation and the analyst's between T (patient) α and T (analyst) α, between T (patient) β and T (analyst) β. I shall abbreviate these signs further to Tp α and Ta α, Tp β and Ta β.

The experiences illustrated in Chapter 2 differ, but the illustrations may not display these differences adequately. The inadequacy lies in notation for the presentation of psycho-analytic phenomena with the precision required.

B has an emotional background which I believe to be typical, though this will need confirmation. From the first, it was evident that the resources of psycho-analysis might prove inadequate to the demands of such a patient. In terms of time and money alone treatment would be costly. Patience and a capacity for taking risks were also soon seen to be necessary. It was only necessary for the patient to feel that one demand was satisfied for him to make it the prelude for further exactions; this attitude pervaded all aspects of relationship with me and apparently with life at large. Typical of the development of awareness of a situation to a point at which I could venture on a verbal impression of it, was the fact that awareness grew gradually so that it was difficult to say, when an aspect had been clarified, what material, in the immediate circumstances, was sufficient to sustain the burden of interpretation I wished to lay on it. An interpretation therefore appeared to lack the scientific quality that is conferred by supporting evidence. I have drawn attention to the high degree of speculation in my second description of B. A series of such doubts sprang naturally from the fact, obvious at the outset, and therefore of slight significance in the immediate analytic setting, that any collaboration, and particularly an analytic one, with such a patient would be unrewarding and even dangerous. Such premonitions have two mainsprings: the first from the analysis itself, which is so transformed that the intention that the analytic association should be healing and rewarding is frustrated by actions intended to wound; the second from perceptions of the patient's material as it coheres to form his representation of O. This first transformation is analogous to that of the landscape gardener who works to transform the landscape itself; the second transformation is analogous to that of the painter who transforms the landscape into a painting. It is doubtful whether the transformation of the analysis into something wounding[1] should be included amongst transformations in the sense in which I have used the term so far. The state of mind in which such behaviour is dominant may be described as the patient studying the interpretations he receives (Ta β). The object of his study is to arrive at action by which he may destroy psycho-analysis. It is a necessary part of the process to arrive by Tp α at Tp β as a prelude to destructive activities, but the transformation does not require special categorization because of the end it is to serve. The danger that the colloquial sense of a "transformation of the analysis" will infect the meaning I wish to reserve for the theory of transformation is one against which I wish to guard by using the sign T. The "transformation of the analysis" refers to a change of "uses" as set out on the horizontal axis of the grid.[2] The subject is one to which I shall return after investigating illustration B.

I shall make three assumptions: (i) that the patient is talking about something (O); (ii) that something, O, has impressed him and that he has transformed the impression by the process represented by Tp α, and (iii) that his representation Tp β is comprehensible.

---

[1] The transformation into action approximates to grid category A6.
[2] See End-paper, and Bion, W. R.: *Elements of Psycho-Analysis* where the grid system is more fully discussed.

According to the theory of transformations the emotional experience gives the analyst the opportunity of deciding whether he is faced by evidence for Tp (that is the impression of O gained by the patient), Tp α, or Tp β. Ideally the analyst should be in the state of mind presented by C_3, C_4, C_5 and D_3, D_4, D_5, with the exception of moments when he intends to give an interpretation. In fact, this is unlikely because the patient's attacks on his state of mind can be incessant and, in my experience, not infrequently successful.[1] Attacks may be generalized and depend for their force on the patient's capacity for being a liability in any situation in which he finds himself. Or they may be given particularity by the evocative use of sundry words such as "police . . . what are you doing?" "My uncle . . . I am saying 'madness' for some reason," and so on, depending on material that has been presented at various times during the analysis. I ignore distraction produced by counter-transference as I have nothing to add to what is already known about it or the methods of dealing with it.

The problem of classifying the material is complicated because it contains elements of all three: Tp, Tp α and Tp β. It is a matter of consequence because the decision depends on what is most convenient for the analyst.[2] If it seems the best approach to interpretation to narrow scrutiny (say C_4 and D_4) to those aspects of the material that are expressions of Tp β the analyst should adjust accordingly. The problem is to reformulate Tp β in conversational, but precise, English. This aim is to produce statements that could be appropriately categorized by the grid category F, or G_1. That is to express a definitory hypothesis. In my second version of B, sundry speculative statements cannot be classified as F_1 or G_1, for that implies too great a degree of scientific sophistication. I suggest the category C_1.

Suppose the approach to be fruitful: this would mean that I was gaining an impression of the patient's picture of some event—O. What, then, is Op?

---

[1] See Chapter 5. p. 54
[2] And the decision the analyst makes is to identify with a particular vertex: see Chapter, 6.

At this point defects in this approach obtrude because the nature of the speculations indicates that the differences of B from A are such that the signs Ta and p, Ta and pα, Ta and pβ are insufficient. Their inadequacy derives from the fact that the combined operation by patient and analyst receives an accession of emotion from the confusion, in the patient's mind, between himself and the analyst. I shall anticipate by marking the difference between the transformation of A with that in B by calling the former a Rigid and the latter a Projective Transformation.

A patient[1] was speaking of problems in his office. But for certain peculiarities which I shall come to in a moment, his account seemed to be realistic, coherent and rational. The peculiarities lay in his response to interpretations. When I referred to something he had just said, a row with his secretary, for example, he would reply blankly "What row?" as if the topic were strange to him. On these occasions there seemed to be nothing that I could say that did not have the effect of leading him away from the theme of his communication and destroying the coherence of the material. About a half of the session was employed in this way and the mood was not replaced by another till I had given a number of interpretations to the effect that his questions showed that the thread in his apparently coherent account was precariously maintained. Every sentence was a series of tenuously connected splits so that if I drew attention to something he mentioned at the beginning of a sentence he had forgotten it by the time he had reached the end; interpretation was made meaningless. My interpretation was based on the assumption that the episode approximated to the Kleinian theory that an attack was being delivered against analytic potency by means of splitting which had the incidental effect of splitting him. Judged by the change of mood and the associated developments, the interpretation appeared to be correct.

Assumption of hostility depended less on the matter of his communication than on the manner and particularly on the peculiarities stressed here. Once the assumption of hostility was made it became possible to see the analytic significance

[1] Referred to later as C.

of the matter he was communicating. The problem depends
for its solution on observation of the patient's behaviour over
a relatively short period and contrasts with the problem of
hostility spread out over a long period and expressed in
episodes of short duration. The individual episode is easier
to deal with than the totality of episodes. In so far as they
are dealt with they contribute to the solution of the whole,
yet the problem of the whole comprises far more than the
sum of the parts. I shall illustrate this by a situation that is
built up over, and endures for, years. In the last chapter I
pointed out that with some patients any association is unrewarding to both associates. This applies to the class of
patient to which the one of whom I am writing belonged.
Consequently such analysis brings about a progressive discrediting of patient, analyst and psycho-analysis in the eyes
of all who know the case socially. Together with this, and
essential to it, is arduous and devoted effort, directed
towards both attendance and work in the session itself. The
essential feature is stimulation and frustration of hope, and
work that is fruitless except in discrediting analyst and
patient. Destructive activity is balanced by enough success
to deny the patient fulfilment of his destructiveness. A
helpful summary of such a case is to describe it as "chronic"
murder of patient and analyst, or, an instance of parasitism;
the main features are dependence of the patient, the parasite,
on analyst and the associated group, or family, or wider
social group. The patient draws on the love, benevolence,
indulgence of the host to extract the knowledge and power
which enables him to poison the association and destroy the
indulgence on which he depends for his existence.

I could give instances, such as example C, which are
essential to the production of this result but which are none
of them individually of obvious consequence; that aspect is
apparent only when they are repeated and then only if seen
to form part of a coherent whole. A total view is possible
for the analyst; the problem, in face of constant splitting
and projective identification is how to make it clear to the
patient. The theory of transformations affords an approach
to a solution in the following way.

First, the problem needs to be stated in terms of the theory. I have at my disposal the following signs: "Invariants", "O", "T", "Tp α", "Ta α", "Tp β", "Ta β". Preceding chapters have indicated the universe of discourse to which they are intended to apply and the domain of that discourse to which each term is assigned. To that extent each sign may be said to represent a meaning. The status of the meaning represented by each sign is indicated by grid category C4;[1] that is to say that the genetic stage of thought is that of dream or myth—the pejorative philosophical expression for a doubtful theory as a mythology—and column 4 that it is to be used to focus attention on appropriate facets[2] of material.

In practice the next development would be dictated by the experience of the session; according to the form taken by it one or more of the signs would become invested with meaning. Reliance on clinical observation for accretion of meanings is central to the use of the theory of transformations. But in this theoretical discussion we may substitute an inquiry into the meaning to be sought for any sign, for the stimulus which would in practice be supplied by the material; no significance is to be attached to the choice I make other than the convenience of exposition. I shall commence with Op and Oa.

The advantage of this is that the facts are limited to the experience shared by patient and analyst.

I shall reduce O to the simplest terms by considering first the facts known to the analyst, Oa. With modifications appropriate to the individual Oa may be said to consist of the following components: two people, patient and analyst, are met together in conditions of privacy. The furniture of the room, remaining unchanged, should be quite familiar to the analyst. The same should be true of features such as the usual sounds of the household and neighbourhood. The familiarity of the surroundings may blind the analyst to the possible significance of them for the patient and he must be on his guard against this. This completes, in general terms, the constant features.

[1] End-paper and Bion, W. R.: *Elements of Psycho-Analysis.*
[2] See vertices, Chapter 6.

Amongst changing features must be listed absence of patient or analyst, or, notably during breaks, of analyst and patient. To these must be added changes in time-table and others likely to be significant. *All* change is a component of O, but one is constant, namely that which flows from the passage of time.

The personality of the analyst is recognized as a feature of the analytic situation but he may not attach enough importance to the strength and weakness of aspects of his personality that are relatively unrelated to psychopathology and have to be learned from experiences other than those of his own analysis.

O, subjected to Ta α, eventuates in Ta β, the analyst's view of himself and extensions of his personality.

Turning to the patient, we find some features of Oa and Op intersect to give Oa and p. Patients vary in what they include in O. In the group of projective transformations, events far removed from any relationship to the analyst are actually regarded as aspects of the analyst's personality. Thus a patient reported angrily that the milkman had called. The patient was angry with me and went into a sulk. For about five minutes he would not talk, but then began to complain about the noise. I knew he was referring to a boy who was whistling cheerfully in the street. I was certain that the milkman had called and that the patient made no distinction between the milkman and myself; conversely, my presence in the consulting room was not distinguished from the milkman's call; this phenomenon differs from transference. A patient might use the milkman's visit to express emotions arising in his relationship with me and it could be interpreted accordingly. That transformation belongs to the set of rigid motions. In this illustration the interpretation might be couched in terms suitable for a transference interpretation and it would probably still be effective. But the difference between rigid motion and projective transformation on other occasions might be important. The importance lies in the fact that the patient believes that the "milkman" me did in fact visit his house and that this same "milkman" me has just appeared to him.

If I do not seem to know about the milkman's visit it makes the patient feel I cannot be aware of my behaviour and am therefore not responsible for my actions—that I am, in short, "mad". Contrasting this with a session where I have to deal with his reactions, say to my absence during a week-end, in the latter instance I know what he is talking about, what Op is, but on other occasions I am confronted with his reaction to Op without knowing what Op might have been —though I can always attempt to guess.

It does not meet the case to suppose that Op, as I am describing it here, is a manifestation of transference for the term "transference" should be reserved for the description of the response to a stimulus; whereas I am concerned to delineate the stimulus. Op, in projective transformations, must not be regarded as identical with Op in rigid motion transformations. The necessity for establishing the nature of the difference springs from the exigencies of psycho-analytic practice. When I assigned O to denote the reality, the impressions of which the individual submits to the process $T\alpha$, I had in mind what Kant describes as the unknowable thing-in-itself. $Tp\,\beta$ or $Ta\,\beta$ denotes the analyst's or patient's representation of what is a private communication understood only by the individual whose processes have effected the transformation. They are thus denoting a representation that is related to what Kant describes as a primary process. If patient and analyst agree on an interpretation the interpretation can be correctly denoted by the sign Tp and Ta β. Since this is shared by two people it is no longer a private communication but has become public. In this respect it is related to what Kant describes as a secondary quality and is by way of qualifying for recognition as common-sense, as I have defined that expression.[1] In rigid motion transformations the invariants establish the relationship with O. But in projective transformations the differences between Op and Oa do not permit of a process of arguing back from Tp and Ta β to Op and Oa as it can be done in rigid motion transformations. The crux lies in the nature of Op in projective transformation. Op is

[1] See Bion, W. R.: *Learning from Experience.*

apparently the stimulus; yet it has qualities which seem to be appropriate to Kant's primary quality. The difficulty becomes less formidable if Op in projective transformation is a psychic reality and has the same capacity for initiating a train of mental events as is possessed by an event of external reality such as a break in the routine of sessions. A feeling of dread might be such an internal psychic reality.

The artist stimulates a reaction in his public by his representation of the subject of his painting. Recognition that a painting depicts a field of poppies depends on invariants common to the original landscape and the representation, to O and $T \beta$. Such an invariant might be that which stimulated, in landscape and painting, the impression of redness. A transformation dependent on a "red-to-red" invariant would not be likely to produce the effect achieved by the "great" artist who produces a "great" painting. The problem is the transformation that issues in an end-product, $T \beta$, which communicates an *emotional* experience, such as the artist intends to produce, in the greatest number of the people in whom he intends to produce it. The components of $T \beta$ in this class of transformation are: emotional experience, precision of communication, universality and durability.

The psycho-analyst tries to help the patient to transform that part of an emotional experience of which he is unconscious into an emotional experience of which he is conscious. If he does this he helps the patient to achieve private knowledge. But since scientific work demands communication of discovery to other workers the psycho-analyst must transform *his* private experience of psycho-analysis so that it becomes a public experience. The artist is used here as a model intended to indicate that the criteria for a psycho-analytic paper are that it should stimulate in the reader the emotional experience that the writer intends, that its power to stimulate should be durable, and that the emotional experience thus stimulated should be an accurate representation of the psycho-analytic experience (Oa) that stimulated the writer in the first place.

It will be observed that in model and psycho-analytic experience the following parallels exist: landscape and psycho-analytic experience, painting and scientific paper, emotions stimulated by landscape and analytic session, emotions represented by painting and scientific paper. We may regard the transformation as extending beyond the limits I have imposed if we consider the progression from O to T β as a link in the progression from O to the emotional state stimulated by T β in the observer of the painting, or the reader of the paper. If the emotion stimulated in the recipient of the communication is a *representation* of the emotion stimulated by O in the artist we may regard the artist's intervention in the chain of events as one that does not stop at the disposal of patterns of pigment on canvas, but extends to the emotional state evoked in the individual, or group, and to giving durability to the power to evoke emotion.[1] The sign T can be made to denote either canvas, or paper, or the emotional state of the recipient of the communication. Our model serves psycho-analytic needs better if T β denotes the emotional state stimulated in the recipient and T represents the emotional state, stimulated in the analyst by O, which Ta α is to transform. The same value must be given to each sign throughout any given universe of discourse; if the universe of discourse is transformation in the domain of emotion, T β, for example, must not at one moment denote canvas and pigment and at another the emotional state of the recipient of the communication.

To bring the discussion into closer approximation to the needs of psycho-analysis—no one can ever know what happens in the analytic session, the thing-in-itself, O; we can only speak of what the analyst or patient *feels* happens, his emotional experience, that which I denote by T. We know what the participants *say* happens, or the emotional state engendered by the verbalization of analyst or patient in the listener. By analogy with the model we must decide whether to use T β to denote (*a*) the verbalization (association or interpretation) or (*b*) the emotional state *produced* by

---

[1] The theme of "Vixere fortes ante Agammemnona multi. . . ." Horace Odes, Bk. IV, 9.

the association or interpretation.[1] Similarly we must decide whether the significance of the association or interpretation lies in its being an emotional response to O or in its intention to evoke or represent an emotional response. If it is the former, then it belongs to the category represented by T. If T, then it is necessary to know whether it is significant because it *is* the emotional response or merely represents it. The model of the artist retains its value, but it may become misleading and lead into paths that are irrelevant; the signs may lack specificity or tend to a proliferation that obscures rather than illuminates. I shall retain both model and signs until something better becomes possible.

To forestall misgivings and criticisms which may have an insidious appeal for the psycho-analyst: a book on psycho-analysis in which the first chapters contain no substantial reference to sexuality, conflict, anxiety, or Oedipus situation, may seem irrelevant, or of specialized interest and minor consequence. In fact, if the matters I am discussing are regarded as seriously as I think they should be, it becomes possible for the analyst to have a firm and durable grasp of the reality of the analytic experience and the theories to which it approximates. The theory of transformations and its development does not relate to the main body of psycho-analytic theory, but to the practice of psycho-analytic *observation*. Psycho-analytic theories, patient's or analyst's statements are representations of an emotional experience. If we can understand the process of representation it helps us to understand the representation and what is being represented. The theory of transformations is intended to illuminate a chain of phenomena in which the understanding of one link, or aspect of it, helps in the understanding of others. The emphasis of this inquiry is on the nature of the transformation in a psycho-analytic session.

T β may be expressed through the medium of speech. Psycho-analysts agree that correct analysis demands that

---

[1] Strictly speaking the interpretation *draws attention* to an *existing* emotional state; but it *produces* the emotional state of awareness of an emotional state. In fact the decision depends on whether we think the analyst or patient works in words or in emotions.

the analyst's interpretation should formulate what the patient's behaviour reveals; conversely, that the analyst's judgment should be embodied in an interpretation[1] and not in an emotional discharge (e.g. counter-transference or acting out). To this we may add provisionally that his contribution may be regarded as embodied in the change in the patient's emotional state.

I shall not discuss transformation in scientific communications except to illustrate transformation in analytic practice.

The analyst conducting a session must decide instinctively the nature of the communication that the patient is making. I suggested, in *Elements of Psycho-Analysis*, a method of classification to aid in developing capacity for such instinctive decisions and have embodied it in the grid.[2] If exigencies of the analysis demand emphasis on the growth of the patient's thought the analyst's attention will dwell mainly on the row that determines the category—the vertical axis. If emphasis is on the use that the patient is making of his communication the analyst's attention will be directed to the horizontal component. The content of the communication, so important in analysis, will be touched on only incidentally in the discussion of transformations; it will depend on O as deduced from the material in the light of the psycho-analyst's theoretical pre-conceptions. Thus, if the content is oedipal material I do not concern myself with this but with the transformation it has undergone, the stage of growth it reveals, and the use to which its communication is being put. This exclusion of content is artificial, to simplify exposition, and cannot be made in practice.

Since I shall refer to phenomena related to Melanie Klein's theories of projective identification, transition from paranoid-schizoid to depressive positions, and vice versa, it may seem that I am concerned primarily with psychotic personalities, but this is not so. These mechanisms are operative in neuroses and psychoses alike. But their investigation is a prime consideration in psychotic disorder, secondary in neuroses. This has been discussed further after elaboration of the theory of transformations[3] has shown the

[1] F1, 3, 4.   [2] See End-papers.   [3] See Chapter 2, p. 15.

possibility of making a fresh distinction between neurosis and psychosis.

To review briefly the points made in this chapter: we must be prepared to find the model of the painter misleading though still useful. The theory of transformations is to be developed, not as an addition to or alteration of psycho-analytic observation. I shall use the grid categories and in particular refer to column 6. This will involve some explana-tion of what I mean by the term, loosely employed, "action" in column 6. I shall start by taking the last point first.

In his paper on "Two Principles of Mental Functioning"[1] Freud distinguishes between a stage where muscular action is taken to alter the environment and a stage when a capacity for thought exists. I propose to include in the category represented by the term "action" phantasies that the mind, acting as if it were a muscle and a muscle acting as a muscle, can disburden the psyche of accretions of stimuli. I include the Kleinian concept of the phantasy known as projective identification in this category of "action". The growth of insight depends, at its inception, on undisturbed functioning of projective identification. If it is disturbed, mental development is hampered by the phantasy that insight depends on what is regarded, even by the sophisticated mind, as action. There are thus two attitudes distinguishable in patients of whom some behave as if action were precedent to action. The first I associate with projective transformations, the second with rigid transforma-tions.

Since there is a breakdown in the early stages of develop-ment of insight many elements[2] involved in projective transformations will be represented by the first row of the grid. The existence of elements A2 and A3 is questionable, but I include them because their exclusion would be equally debatable.

Elements and objects in rigid transformations are likely to be found in all grid categories.

[1] Freud, S.: "Two Principles of Mental Functioning" (1911). Standard Edition, Vol. XII.
[2] See Bion, W. R.: *Elements of Psycho-Analysis*.

CHAPTER FOUR

THEORY leaves us free to give Ta β the value of the analyst's verbalization of his experience in the session, or the emotional state induced in his patient. That the analyst works on his patient's emotions as a painter might work on his canvas would be repugnant to psycho-analytic theory and practice. The painter who works on his public's emotions with an end in view is a propagandist with the outlook of the poster artist. He does not intend his public to be free in its choice of the use to which it puts the communication he makes. The analyst's position is akin to that of the painter who by his art adds to his public's experience. Since psycho-analysts do not aim to run the patient's life but to enable him to run it according to his lights and therefore to know what his lights are, Ta β either in the form of interpretation or scientific paper should represent the psycho-analyst's verbal representation of an emotional experience. An attempt to exclude by restriction to verbal expression any element from Ta that would make it pass from the domain of communication of knowledge to propaganda would be inadequate. Verbal expression must be limited so that it expresses truth without any implication other than the implication that it is true in the *analyst's opinion*. How this is to be attempted lies outside the scope of this discussion, but for certain implications which I shall now consider. The first concerns the route by which we have arrived at this conclusion. It is sometimes assumed that the motive for scientific work is an abstract love for truth. The argument I have followed implies that the grounds for limiting the values that may be substituted for Ta β to true statements lies in the nature of values *not* so limited and their relationship to other components in the T theory. If truth is not essential to all values of Ta β, Ta β must be regarded as expressed in and by manipulation of the emotions of patient or public and not in or by the interpretation; truth is essential for any value of Ta β in art or science. How is truth to be a criterion

for a value proposed to Ta β? To what has it to be true
and how shall we decide whether it is or not? Almost any
answer appears to make truth contingent on some circumstance or idea that is itself contingent. Falling back on
analytic experience for a clue, I am reminded that healthy
mental growth seems to depend on truth as the living
organism depends on food. If it is lacking or deficient the
personality deteriorates. I cannot support this conviction by
evidence regarded as scientific. It may be that the formulation belongs to the domain of Aesthetic. In practice the
problem arises with schizoid personalities in whom the
super-ego appears to be developmentally prior to the ego
and to deny development and existence itself to the ego.
The usurpation by the super-ego of the position that should
be occupied by the ego involves imperfect development of
the reality principle, exaltation of a "moral" outlook and
lack of respect for the truth. The result is starvation of the
psyche and stunted growth. I shall regard this statement as
an axiom that resolves more difficulties than it creates.

The medium in which the psycho-analyst works is verbalized thoughts. Using the grid[1] to categorize the verbalized
thoughts more precisely, they should be true and fall within
the categories of rows E, F, and possibly D and G, and
columns 1, 3, 4 and 5. Row G and H apply to phenomena
endowed with a greater degree of sophistication and precision than any to which psycho-analysis attains at present.
If the statements made in the course of interpretation are
expressions of feeling they should fall in the same categories.
The patient's contribution is not restricted and may fall in
any grid category; the grid categories are intended to be
adequate for all the elements and psycho-analytic objects
met with in the practice of psycho-analysis. They should
therefore be adequate for the requirements of a theory of
transformations.

By considering psycho-analytic experience in the light of[2]
a theory of transformations it is possible to see the problems

---

[1] See End-papers and Bion, W. R.: *Elements of Psycho-Analysis.*
[2] Or, with a vertex having the value T. See Chapter 6.

of thinking afresh. Freud associated thinking with the dominance of the reality principle and showed that it interposed a stage between awareness of an impulse and the action necessary for its fulfilment; he drew attention to its ameliorating effect on frustration. Its absence exacerbates frustration. Transformations have a number of functions, such as notation and record, private and public communication and the pursuit of knowledge; I shall consider an aspect of the latter, seeking an analogy with mathematics for the purpose.

A mathematical illustration is afforded by the use of numbers for enumeration and record. An increase in sophistication marks the manipulation of numbers to solve a problem *in the absence of the objects giving rise to the problem.* Applying this analogy to the elements of psycho-analysis, as I have categorized them in the grid, it is evident that an advance in sophistication separates the categories of columns 1 and 3 from the categories in all other columns. A distinction must be made between categories in column 2 and those of columns 4 to n-1, n, but in this case the distinction is one of kind, not sophistication.

Columns 1 and 3 represent uses of a relatively simple kind; if a word, hypothesis, theoretical system, myth, or transformation were limited to uses represented by those columns, it would not be suitable for working with. An analyst's notes on his cases are useless for the statement of problems and adumbration of solutions if their form prevents extension beyond definition and record. The theory of transformations must serve to illuminate and solve the problems that lie unsolved at the heart of certain forms of mental disturbance; and to do the same for problems inherent in the psychoanalysis of such disturbances.

A theory of transformations must be composed of elements and constitute a system capable of the greatest number of uses (represented by the horizontal axis of the grid) if it is to extend the analyst's capacity for working on a problem with or without the material components of the problem present.

This may seem to introduce a dangerous doctrine opening

the way for the analyst who theorizes unhampered by the facts of practice, but the theory of transformations is inapplicable to any situation in which observation is not an essential. Observation is to be made and recorded in a form suitable for working *with* but inimical to wayward and undisciplined fabrications. As grid categories show any scientific theory can be used in accordance with the categories of column 2 but it may be possible to prevent unpredictable changes from the uses of one grid column to the uses of another. In short, the theory is to aid observation and recording in terms suitable for scientific manipulation without the presence of the objects.

One problem in analysing the psychotic patient seems to be his difficulty in working without the actual presence of the objects for and about which work must be done.[1] If we could suppose that there was a failure to develop a system of notation and record which could also be used for manipulation in the absence of the object it might explain a number of features associated with the psychotic's behaviour. I have noticed that he sometimes behaves as if in order to "think" something he had to wait for that thing to appear in the world of external reality. Similarly he seems unable to think or imagine a situation but has to act it out. Stating this in terms of a theory of transformation the patient is not able to transform T (the phenomenal counterpart of O) into $Tp\,\beta$. Indeed he talks as if he felt unable to transform O into T. It is as if in one view man can never know the thing-in-itself, but only secondary and primary qualities; whereas in the other view he can never "know" anything *but* the thing-in-itself. This apparent attitude has similarities with another apparent attitude, namely, that postulated by the theory of projective identification. He behaves as if parts of his personality had physical properties and could be split off and projected into others as physical objects which the other object could modify or use.[2] Since a psychotic

---

[1] Hence the tendency to produce problem situations instead of solving problems.

[2] See Klein, M.: "Notes on Some Schizoid Mechanisms." In: *Developments in Psycho-Analysis*.

patient can express words and sentences it seems reasonable to suppose that he can think. But thinking, in the sense of manipulating words and thoughts to do work in the absence of the object, seems to be just what the patient cannot do. I have said[1] that such patients do not have memories but only undigested facts. The breakdown appears to occur in the necessity for an object into which the patient feels he is able to project parts of his personality for their development and manipulation. If he feels there is no such object, and no such possibility as "splitting off parts of his personality" disturbance is set up.

The use of transformation to produce T β such that T β can be worked with in the absence of O is one aspect of transformation theory. The theory must be extended to be adequate to cover transformation of this kind and the projective transformations of which I spoke earlier.

The similarity of phenomena associated with the theory of projective identification to those associated with lack of any differentiation of thing from its corresponding thought is probably due to their being different aspects of the same state of mind.

If the apparent inability to transform O to T corresponds to a real inability it would mean an end to the discussion— no theory of transformations could apply as no transformations take place. I have, however, deliberately described the patient as talking *as if* he could not transform O to T so as to leave the matter open to discussion; patients who show, or appear to show, this disability are in fact able to communicate with the analyst. The communication, though words are used, is more akin to musical or artistic than verbal communication. It contrasts with what I have said (on pages 24–26) about the nature of Ta β, the analyst's contribution.

Ordinary language is already more than a method of recording and enables work to be done, like mathematics, in the absence of the object worked on, but it is less effective in precision and universality. So long as our communications are reliable only in the presence of the objects we study,

[1] See Bion, W. R.: *Learning from Experience.*

we work under disabilities analogous to those of the psychotic and quality must suffer correspondingly. The theory of transformations is designed to decrease the disabilities of the psycho-analyst in his study of similar disabilities in the patient. I propose therefore to study alternately the transformations of the patient and the transformations of the analyst with a view to formulating a theory of transformations superior to those already used consciously and unconsciously.

The next task will be to examine afresh the group that I have provisionally called projective transformations. In this group Tp β appears to require two personalities, an object into which something is to be projected and an object responsible for the projection. Associated with this is the problem of deciding what the nature of Tp β is, if the object, into which the projection is made, is missing.

The mathematician in the absence of other than mathematical objects can work with his notation and formulations to solve a specific problem. To some extent the analyst can do the same with verbal communications; he can work with a patient, transform his experience into words, communicate his results to patient, or make them available to another analyst who can in turn use them and the work already done, in his task with a new patient and a new problem. Work has thus been done, in the absence of a patient, to carry forward the solution of a *general* problem and make it available for *specific* use in a specific instance. This can be likened to the process whereby growth[1] has been promoted, from the state represented by the earlier rows in the grid, to the state represented by row D. Such a transformation of the communication fits it for one of the uses in the horizontal axis, in this instance, column 4.

This description is of a characteristic common to several types of mental growth. Starting with the simplest example discussed, namely, from the name of an object, and

---

[1] "Growth" here refers to the growth of a mental formulation. It is interesting to consider the relationship that exists when the growth of a mental formulation appears to be matched by a realization of growth that approximates, or is "parallel" to, the mental formulations.

proceeding to quite complex combinations of objects, the growth process can be described as passing through a number of stages from β-element to algebraic calculus. Each stage is a record of a previous stage and a pre-conception of the subsequent stage. Each stage can be used in ways indicated in the headings of the horizontal axis. Each "use" represented in the horizontal axis can be seen to be representable by a term used to represent a stage on the genetic axis. "Pre-conception" can represent equally the use which is being made of a statement and the genetic stage of the statement. It is therefore appropriate to ask if the investigation would gain and the grid be improved by bringing stages and uses into clearer approximation to each other. Thus columns 4 and 5 might be amalgamated and be represented by the term "pre-conception". The term would then denote a use, but in the vertical axis it would continue to represent a stage in growth. But if each stage can be regarded as an element that is both record and pre-conception it may be objected that there is no need for terms such as "β-element", "dream", "concept", etc. In practice this is not so; it is useful for psycho-analysis to be able to signify degrees of growth and to represent these by stages with their proper sign.

Hitherto I have spoken of "growth" and "increased sophistication" when speaking of the progression from A to H; is it possible to give more precise meaning to these terms? I shall consider some possibilities.

Growth from elements of one row to the row next below cannot very well be measured by an increase in the "uses" (represented by the columns of the horizontal axis) to which the element can be put for I have already supposed that any element in its character as member of a row also can have a character derived from its membership of any column of the horizontal axis and in practice it is useful to retain this supposition. An approximation to universality of uses to which a row can be put is therefore unlikely to provide a criterion for growth. It may be that some rows are better suited to serve a multiplicity of uses than others. Similarly some uses may be served more effectively by some rows than by others. For example, I have said that β-elements lend themselves to projective identification when that mechanism is employed to evacuate a part of the personality, but are useless, or at best extremely unsuited, for use in thinking—which is to say for any use other than those of columns 2 and 6. A possible approach may therefore be provided by considering the nature of the match between the stage (or row) and the use matching row and column in terms of the appropriateness of one to the other, but this only shelves the problem by postponing it to a later stage in the discussion, for it necessitates criteria by which to judge appropriateness. Some of the pitfalls are less dangerous in the practice of analysis than they are in an abstract discussion of the problems. Thus in practice it is easier to feel that β-elements are not appropriate to thinking than to discuss in the abstract a criterion for the appropriate. Herein lies one advantage that the psycho-analyst possesses over the philosopher; his statements can be related to realizations and realizations to a psycho-analytic theory. What psycho-analytic thinking requires is a method of notation and rules for its employment that will enable work to be done in the *absence* of the object, to facilitate further work in the *presence* of the object. The barrier to this that is presented by unfettered play of an analyst's phantasies has long been recognized: pedantic statement on the one hand and verbalization loaded with unobserved implications on the other mean that the potential for misunderstanding and erroneous deduction is so high as to vitiate the value of the work done with such defective tools. I would retain the freedom to speak of "incorporating" a particular theory "in the main body of analytic theory", with the precision necessary for use[1] of Melanie Klein's theories of internal objects. This means that there must be psycho-analytic invariants, of which I have already written, psycho-analytic variables, and psycho-analytic parameters. These mathematical terms, used in this sentence as models, row C, need transformation to fit them for psycho-analytic use as row F, G and H elements.

1 Columns 1, 3 and 4.

By writing "psycho-analytic" invariants, variables and parameters I have limited the universe of discourse; only within this universe of discourse can these terms be described as representing invariants or parameters. There is opportunity for ambiguity if this is not recognized; the term "variable" may describe something which, in a particular universe of discourse, is given a constant value and so qualifies for description as a parameter (as in a mathematical formulation, say $ax + by - c = 0$, the signs a, b, c, representing variables are given constant value).

According to Heisenberg, in atomic physics a situation has arisen in which the scientist cannot rely on the ordinarily accepted view that the researcher has access to facts, because the facts to be observed are distorted by the very act of observation. Furthermore, the field in which he has to observe the relationship of one phenomenon to another is unlimited in extent, and yet none of the phenomena "in" that field can be ignored because all interact. It follows that the fact that the universe of discourse is finite is not matched by a corresponding fact in the relationship to each other of the realizations supposedly approximating to the universe of discourse. The universe of discourse itself must always be defined (thus falling into the categories of grid column 1) if its terms are to have meaning. Yet, by virtue of this very fact it becomes of doubtful validity unless it is realized that to the finite universe of discourse no realization corresponds.

The point may not be of immediate importance, but it may be a source of error and it *is* a part of the psycho-analyst's methodological problem. The situation of the psycho-analyst dealing with psychotic transformations is similar to that attributed to nuclear physicists. He has to deal with relationships of a domain that has no finite limitations. The terms psycho-analytic invariant, variable and parameter are meaningful in a universe of discourse that has in one important respect no realization corresponding to it; his interpretations have characteristics of relatedness that are applicable to his universe of discourse, but not to the phenomena they represent, since those phenomena possess a relatedness, if there is one, appropriate to an infinite universe. If a patient says that he knows that his "char" is in league with the postman because his friend left white of egg in the bathroom the relatedness implied by his statement may differ from forms of relatedness to which I am accustomed because his statement represents phenomena related to each other in an infinite universe.

Freud made a statement, which is similar in principle, when he adumbrated the universe of discourse in which conscious behaviour is studied by postulating an unconscious, but the characteristics of *relatedness* remain unchanged in the new universe of discourse. The differentiating factor that I wish to introduce is not between conscious and unconscious, but between finite and infinite. Nevertheless I use, as my model for forms of relatedness in an infinite universe, forms of relatedness operative in a finite universe of discourse and its approximate realization. It follows therefore that the model is likely to be faulty.

When I used the concrete elements of a transformation (namely the subject stimulating the artist) at one end of the chain of events and the finished painting at the other, I did so to provide a model for a part of the whole—the part that takes place in the mind of the artist. The psycho-analyst's domain is that which lies between the point where a man receives sense impressions and the point where he gives expression to the transformation that has taken place. The principles of this investigation must be the same whether the medium is painting, music, mathematics, sculpture, or a relationship between two people, whether expressed verbally or by any other means. These principles must be determined so that they remain constant whether the transformation is effected in a mind which is sane or insane.

I take an illustration from an analysis in which the patient had considerable adjustment to reality. He entered the room, and, avoiding my glance, walked to the couch and lay down while I was going to my chair. On these facts, as it appeared in the session, there was agreement between us, but he showed great anxiety and told me that he felt, when walking to the couch, that I was attacking his genitalia from behind. He was able to tell me that this was as real to him as the agreed facts. He did not know why he was anxious. That, as near as I can make it so, is a correct account of what took place and is my transformation (Ta β) of what took place (O). Is it advantageous to regard this episode as a transformation and, if so, in what respect?

I propose to consider this episode in detail though in analysis this was not, and could not be, possible. I shall use the proposals I have made in *Learning from Experience, Elements of Psycho-Analysis,* and the preceding chapters of this book.

The discussion has a two-fold aim; to carry the investigation further and to give an example, in doing so, of my method of applying my methods. First I shall divest myself of pre-conceptions approximating to the state of naivety[1] which translate roughly into words: "*not* knowing to make room for a pre-conception that will illuminate a problem that excites my curiosity."

A lake in calm bright weather reflects trees upon the bank on the shore opposite the observer. The image presented by the trees is transformed in the reflection: a whole series of transformations is effected by atmospheric changes. Suppose the observer could see only the reflection; he would be able to deduce the nature of O from what he saw. Provided conditions were not too disturbed, the demands on the observer's deductive powers would be relatively simple if he were expected only to recognize that he observed the reflection of trees, more difficult if he were called upon to pronounce on the species of tree and impossible if he were to state the nature of microscopical features of leaf structure.

The change in atmosphere from light to darkness or from calm to turbulence would influence the transformation sometimes slightly, at others so deeply that the observer would have to exercise all his perceptiveness to deduce the nature of O. Just as the demands on him could be impossibly exacting so that atmospheric conditions could be impossibly distorting.

I shall use this as a model for the analytic observation of

[1] See *Elements of Psycho-Analysis,* p. 86.

transformations. It will be convenient to suppose that the L, H, K links influence the transformation in a manner analogous to the atmospheric changes in the model: convenient, but not necessarily true, as will be obvious by reference to analytic experience when the emotional tie is extremely complex; so are atmospheric conditions. I do not suggest that turbulence and distortion are invariably the outcome of emotion, but wish to leave myself free to consider the situation when emotions might provide a constant and the variations might be due to some other factor.

In the model, the trees at the lake-side are supposed to be the manifestation of O. What is the nature of the counterpart of O in analysis? Can we suppose that it is invariably a fact known to analyst and analysand, or at least knowable to both? In fact there is no choice in the matter, for if we postulate that O might be *any* circumstance in the patient's life whether known to the analyst or not we postulate a condition that makes analysis impossible. There *are* such facts, but analytic effectiveness depends on their being irrelevant to the analytic procedure or relevant only in so far as some aspect of such a fact *is* available to both analyst and analysand. I therefore postulate that O in any analytic situation is available for transformation by analyst and analysand equally.

I shall ignore disturbance produced by the analyst's personality or aspects of it. The existence of such disturbance is well known and its recognition is the basis for analytic acceptance of the need for analysts to be analysed and the many studies of counter-transference. While other scientific disciplines recognize the personal equation, or the factor of personal error, no science other than psycho-analysis has insisted on such a profound and prolonged investigation of its nature and ramifications. I ignore it therefore so as to keep an already over-complicated problem down to its simplest terms. I shall assume an ideal analyst and that $\text{Ta}\,\alpha$ and $\text{Ta}\,\beta$ are not distorted by turbulence—though turbulence and its sources are part of O.

To summarize the preceding discussion:

1. In psycho-analysis any O not common to analyst and

analysand alike, and not available therefore for transformation by both, may be ignored as irrelevant to psycho-analysis. Any O not common to both is incapable of psycho-analytic investigation; any appearance to the contrary depends on a failure to understand the nature of psycho-analytic interpretation.

2. Transformation, i.e. Tp α or Ta α, is influenced by L, H and K. The analyst is assumed to allow for or exclude L or H from his link with the patient and Ta α and Ta β are assumed for purposes of this discourse to be free from distortion by L, H (i.e. by counter-transference). Tp α and Tp β, on the contrary, are assumed always to be subject to distortion and the nature of that distortion, in so far as it is an object of illumination through psycho-analytic interpretation, is the O of the transformation that the analyst effects in his progress from observation to interpretation. This brings me to consider whether or not it is possible to put a further limitation on what must be considered to lie in the domain of O in psycho-analysis; so far I have suggested O must be available to Ta α and Tp α and to this have added that the transformation of the patient must always be the O that is transformed when the analyst works to arrive at an interpretation. But the analyst must have a view of the psycho-analytic theory of the Oedipus situation. His understanding of that theory can be regarded as a transformation of that theory and in that case all his interpretations, verbalized or not, of what is going on in a session may be seen as transformations of an O that is bi-polar. One pole of O is trained intuitive capacity transformed to effect its juxtaposition with what is going on in the analysis and the other is in the facts of the analytic experience that must be transformed to show what approximation the realization has to the analyst's preconceptions—the preconception here being identical with Ta β as the end-product of Ta α operating on the analyst's psycho-analytic theories.

Freud stated as one of the criteria by which a psychoanalyst was to be judged was the degree of understanding allegiance he paid to the theory of the Oedipus complex. He thus showed the importance he attached to this theory and time has done nothing to suggest that he erred by over-estimation; evidence of the Oedipus complex is never absent though it can be unobserved.

Melanie Klein, in her paper on "Early Phases of the Oedipus Complex", made observations of Oedipal elements where their presence was previously undetected; methods of observation, notation and record, should make failure to detect relevant material less frequent. Part of the equipment of observation is pre-conception used for preconception—$D4$. It is in its $D4$ aspect that I wish to consider the Oedipal theory; that is, as part of the observational equipment of the analyst. The behaviour which this apparatus, "Oedipus complex $D4$", is to scrutinize bears qualities of rows A and B.

But now, difficulties. The first step seems simple enough: to set out the theoretical apparatus with which I shall investigate the material. The theories with which I propose to investigate the patient's material should, in accordance with the theories in the previous part of this book, be described as transformations of the experience of training and learning that I have had. They may be denoted by the sign Ta β of $O1$, $O1$ here being the stimulus provided by my accumulation of experience, and Ta β of $O2$, $O2$ being the experience of the session I am investigating. Ta β, the end product of my transformation of theories that were passed on to me in personal analysis and training, can now be categorized, according to the degree of sophistication with which it is expressed, as belonging to columns 1, 3, 4, 5, and rows D to F. But the state of free-floating attention, usually regarded as desirable in the analyst, is the more effective the more it approximates to being represented by a wide spectrum of grid categories. Therefore the analyst's state of mind should not be limited to categories $E4$ and $F4$, say, but rather to the area of categories $C \rightarrow F$ by 1, 3, 4, 5. In practice this means that the analyst should be cognizant of dreams in which patients appear, though his interpretation of the significance of their appearance will relate more to their characteristics as column 2 phenomena than to their significance as evidence of his own psychopathology.

The analyst's theoretical equipment may thus be narrowly described D4, E4, F4, but the state of mind in which the theories are available in the session should cover a wider spectrum of the grid. With this proviso in mind I propose to limit the following description of theories to statements that fall in the categories E1, E3, E4 and E5. I mean to employ the following theories:

(1) The theory of projective identification and splitting; mechanisms by which the breast provides what the patient later takes over as his own apparatus for α-function.

(2) The theory that some personalities cannot tolerate frustration.

(3) The theory that a personality with a powerful endowment of envy tends to denude its objects by both stripping and exhaustion.

(4) The theory that at an early stage (or on a primitive level of mind) the oedipal situation is represented by part objects.

(5) The Kleinian theory of envy and greed.

(6) The theory that primitive thought springs from experience of a non-existent object, or, in other terms, of the *place* where the object is expected to be, but is not.

(7) The theory of violence in primitive functions.

As I have already written of these theories in *Learning from Experience* and *Elements of Psycho-Analysis* I shall say no more of them here. These theories, as extensions of the oedipal situation, must be present in the analyst's mind in a form that enables them to be represented in a wide range of grid categories.

I shall now consider phenomena that the state of expectation represented by these theories might be expected to reveal. One difficulty, of those to which I referred on page 5, concerns the communication of material from an experience that is ineffable; the scientific approach, as ordinarily understood, is not available and an aesthetic approach requires an artist. Therefore the reader will need to be indulgent if he is to grasp the meaning I wish to convey; he will find the clinical experience, if it comes his way, simpler than my description makes it appear.

The external stimulus, O, is provided by an impending break of sufficient duration to excite more powerful reactions than those observed at weekends. I knew envy and intolerance of frustration to be powerful factors in the analytic situation and that violence was a prominent function in the patient's personality; he feared violence, his own and other people's; his emotions were violent, his ambitions violently pursued and obstructed, his course of action violently maintained. His thought processes were extremely disturbed, many of his utterances being incomprehensible even after prolonged analysis. When I thought I grasped his meaning it was often by virtue of an aesthetic rather than a scientific experience. There were short-lived lucid communications in which words and syntax were combined in a conventional manner. My own theoretical pre-dispositions I have already indicated. For reasons of discretion references to actual clinical material will be few, and drawn from more than one patient, but this I believe will not produce distortion in matter relevant to the discussion. I shall draw on a wide range of illustration, including historical matter, to fill gaps that I cannot leave without obscurity or fill without disclosure of private matter.

CHAPTER FIVE

THE patient's reaction to O is primitive with material belonging to the categories of rows A and B.

His presence shows that he knows that *I* am present. This fact is used, conformably with column 2 categories, to deny my *absence*. He reacts in the session as if I were absent. This behaviour, in accordance with column 2 categories, is intended to deny my *presence*. Though "absence" and "presence" are each characteristic of column 2 they are brought together at this stage in the analysis, in accordance with A4 and B4 categories.[1]

The state of mind I have described is represented for me by a model—that of an adult who *violently* maintains an exclusively primitive omnipotent ↔ helpless state. The model by which I represent *his* "vision" of *me* is that of an absent breast, the place or position, that I, the breast, *ought* to occupy but do not. The "ought" expresses *moral* violence and omnipotence. The visual image of me can be represented by what a geometer might call a point, a musician the staccato mark in a musical score. As this attitude is important I shall deal with it in detail, using ideas expressed earlier in the book.

The name given an object, often regarded as the sign for a quality abstracted from something,[2] or from which something has been abstracted,[2] is by me defined as genetically related to a selected fact. It is a sign intended to mark, and bind, a constant conjunction. It is therefore significant, but devoid of meaning.[3] It receives its accretion of meaning from experience. It is similar to a theory in that both imply that certain qualities are constantly conjoined; therefore, it cannot properly be described as true or false in its relationship to O; these terms express judgements on the health-giving effect of the theory to which they are applied, upon the

---

[1] Second cycle of transformation.
[2] See Paton, H. J.
[3] Compare Russell, B. *Principles of Mathematics*, Chap. XXVII.

personality entertaining the theory. The differentiation to
be made to the name, or theory, is between "useful" and
"not useful"; it can be categorized according to the terms
of the $1 - n$ axis.

Implicit in the name as that which signifies constant
conjunction, and inseparable from this significance, is the
quality of negation. A constant conjunction, thus bound by
a name, is *not* whatever the personality has observed as
existing previously, but may be similar to it. This has been
a cause of difficulty as far back as Aristotle.[1] In practice it
presents difficulty to the patient who cannot tolerate frustration, and in whom envy, greed and cruelty are dominant.

In the illustration the problem centres on the fact that the
absent breast, the "no-breast", differs from the breast. If
this is accepted the "no-breast" can be represented by the
visual image of the point. But if this is a column 2 phenomenon the point lacks the quality of a definitory statement
and approximates to an object with column 3 characteristics.
It therefore has the meaning that it is a breast that has been
reduced to a mere position—the place where the breast was.
This state appears to the patient to be a consequence either
of greed that has exhausted the breast, or of splitting that
has destroyed the breast leaving only the position.

The patient's relationship with himself is prejudiced if he
cannot advance to recognition of a new experience and so
falls back on existing meaning, or *does* progress and has to
face frustration he cannot tolerate. He can decide, if such
a term is permissible in this context, whether to make
destructive attacks on his link with his object and so destroy
his embryonic thought processes, or to tolerate it and allow
his apparatus for thought to develop. A patient with the
characteristics postulated will be likely to suffer disturbances
of thought either way, for acceptance of the "no-breast"
confronts him with the problem of what to do with the
attendant "thoughts". The problem does not exist in one
dimension only; tolerance of frustration involves awareness
of the presence or absence of objects, and of what a developing personality later comes to know as "time" and (as I

[1] Aristotle: *Topics*, VI.6, 143 b 11 (p. 158).

have described the "position" where the breast used to be) "space".

The factors that reduce the breast to a point, reduce time to "now". Time is denuded of past and future. The "now" is subjected to attacks similar to those delivered against space, or more precisely, the point. It is both exhausted and split. This leads to expressions which can mislead for such a patient will say "at the moment" when he means "never" and "yesterday" or "tomorrow" when he means a split-off fragment of "now"; such beliefs contribute to the problems of a patient who cannot tolerate staccato markings in a musical score.

To turn now to the problems that await the personality that can accept "thoughts". As I have said, the definitory aspect of the name can be seen to have a negative foundation, that is, *not* a, b, c, etc.; or significance without meaning (thereby taking on the uses of column 4, the counterpart in "use" of what I have called, in the genetic axis of the grid, a pre-conception).

The "thoughts" can be combined with other "thoughts" in accordance with rules of syntax if they are verbally stated, rules of mathematical manipulation, if they are mathematically stated, or rules of musical composition if musically stated. But such rules are easier to conceive of in an advanced state of mental development than in the primitive domain with which I am dealing here and I shall leave the discussion of rules of combination on one side till later.[1]

According to Proclus, objection was raised against the term στιγμη by Plato on the grounds that it meant puncture and therefore suggested a background of reality that was not appropriate to geometric discussion. The objection resembles that of a patient to the visual image of the point because of its unwelcome penumbra of associations. He had evaded the difficulty by a neologism; my concern is not with the solution of the problem, but with its resemblance to the scientific difficulty of using terms with a long history to express novel situations.

The Pythagoreans regarded the point as having position,

[1] See Chapter 10, p. 133.

but Euclid did not include this in his definition, though he and Archimedes and later writers used the term σημετον instead of στιγμή; Aristotle in discussing the prevalent notion of the relatedness of the point to the line objected that, the point being indivisible, no accumulation of points can give anything divisible such as a line.[1] The significance of the discussion lies in the wish to establish the connection felt to exist between the point and the line. An analyst reading contributions to the establishment of scientific geometry would see that elements appear that invite psycho-analytic interpretation of the kind indicated. I shall have reason to quote illustrations that strengthen the impression of the sexual component in the mathematical investigation, but I do not propose to go into this aspect of geometric history.

Granted that a patient is capable of visual images, repre-sented by the words "point" and "line", two apparently divergent courses appear to be open to him; he can *think* them, that is, use thoughts in accordance with rules which are acceptable to, and understandable by, others. This leads to the proliferation of a range of statements that fall into grid categories H1, H3, H4, etc. (I ignore H2, though that is possible also) and ultimately to the scientific structures of modern mathematics. *Or*, he *cannot* think them (if we exclude splitting, exhaustion and projection or evacuation as outside what is ordinarily meant by thought) and does not elaborate or employ rules of combination and manipu-lation that are widely acceptable. Such a patient, as in an instance quoted by Segal,[2] has no difficulty in seeing that a man playing a violin is masturbating in public: the fact that he is giving a public performance on the violin is significant, in the sense I have given the term, and it has a meaning, but the meaning it has for him is not the same as the meaning which it has for the ordinary person who regards the performer's activity as a part of music. The ordinary view of it as a musical activity is as alien to him as his view is to the ordinary person. Why then, to revert to the point and

[1] *Physics*, IV, 8, 215, big.
[2] Segal, H.: *Introduction to the work of Melanie Klein.*

line, do these visual images lead in one case to the efflores-
cence of mathematics and in the other to mental sterility?
And is it certain that "mental sterility" is a correct assessment? The question implies the validity of a theory of
causation which I consider misleading and liable to give rise
to constructions that are basically false; if it is fallacious we
may discard it for one as fallacious—which may be true of
the formulation, by Heisenberg,[1] of the problem of multiple
causation. Both views have proved of value in the development of science, but developments of physics by the Copen-
hagen school appear to have made the theory irrelevant. If
so, the logical step would be to bother no longer with
causation or its counterpart—results. In psycho-analysis it
is difficult to avoid feeling that a gap is left by its disappear-
ance and that the gap should be filled. Over a wide range
of our problems no difficulty is caused by regarding the
theory of causation as fallacious, but useful. When it comes
to problems presented by disturbances in thought the
difficulty cannot be met in this way. For though it is
possible, as in the chain of reasoning I have reported,[2] to
see that the patient has a theory of causation that requires
assessment, such assessment cannot be made without contrasting it with some other theory—presumably the analyst's
own.

Melanie Klein's theory of the part played by intolerance
of depression illuminates the problem presented by the chain
of causation I have reported.[2] The patient is persecuted by
the meaning of certain facts that he feels to be significant.
Further, he is persecuted by the feelings of persecution. This
is explicable if we accept that the patient is intolerant of
depression and that this hinders the Ps ↔ D interchange.
The proposed chain of causation can then be seen as a
rationalization of the sense of persecution. Furthermore, if
the patient is capable of seeing that his proposed chain of
causation is nonsensical he may use it to deny the persecution and thus evade any explanation that would reveal the
depression that he dreads.

[1] Heisenberg, W.: *Physics and Philosophy.*
[2] Chapter 4 above.

In putting forward such a suggestion I am postulating a chain of causation in the phenomena I witnessed. I shall risk being misled by an inadequate theory and suggest, as I did in the actual analysis, that the fear of depression depends on the dominance in the patient of a cruel super-ego.

I shall employ mythology to clarify the next stage in my discussion. In terms of the grid I use thought that belongs to the category C_4, and in particular the myth (Eden) that an omniscient and harsh god, opposed to knowledge, is dominant. The Babel myth of the god that confounds language, or the myth of fate attending the Sphinx in the Oedipus myth would serve equally well.

The logical formulation of the problem points to a conflict between omniscience on the one hand and inquiry on the other. Further steps will show that the logical causal approach produces a circular argument. Is there any objection to this and, if so, is there an approach that is better? We have to consider not the patient's "theory of causation" only but that of the analyst also. As the problem is methodological psycho-analytic findings on all that touches learning cannot be separated from it.

The patient in the illustration was attempting to convince himself, or me, of the validity of a causal chain as something to which reason automatically owed allegiance. I was invited to collude with him in agreeing that this particular causal chain was valid. And "valid" in this context meant "not requiring scrutiny". This interpretation is my assessment of the emotional scene in which I was witness and participant. It is an experience that cannot be understood by any that have not experienced it and I cannot demonstrate that the account given represents the facts accurately but at some future date an experience, mine or another's, might approximate to this description.

The accounts that I have given, and the one that I am about to give, might be described as "theories" of what took place. In view of the associations that belong to the term "theory" I prefer the term "transformation". The accounts I give of this episode are transformations in the sense that I have given the term in Chapter 1 and subsequently. The reader may use the grid for evaluating the transformations printed in this book. My overt aim is to write something that could correctly be described as falling within the categories F_1, 3, 4, 5; but the reader may assess them differently and attach different grid categories to the communication according to the facets that he sees.

To return to the episode: in the session the patient was passing rapidly from one visual image to another. In so far as the visual images were parts of his own personality he was identifying himself first with one and then with another. They could not be synthesized; that is to say, he could not allow himself the experience of the selected fact which gives coherence to elements not previously seen to be coherent. Nor could he dismiss the persecuting elements so long as he could not permit coherence. The chain of causation was designed with the express purpose of preventing coherence. But the feeling of persecution itself becomes a persecution, this persecution being "bound" by the idea of a cause. In this context the term "cause" and the associated theory of causation relates not to external reality but psychic reality. The source of anxiety in the patient is his fear of depression and an associated fear of the $Ps \leftrightarrow D$ interchange, the mechanisms of the selected fact. I categorize the idea of cause, in this context, as D_2, that is, a relatively primitive pre-conception used to prevent the emergence of something else. The patient's communication in so far as it is to be described as logical, is a circular argument, supposedly based on a theory of causation, employed to destroy contact with reality, not to further it. In this respect it qualifies for one of Freud's criteria for psychosis—hatred of reality. But the reality that is hated is the reality of an aspect of the patient's personality.[1]

To avoid complexity and the risk of confusion, I shall assume that my interpretations were governed by the need to establish my own and the patient's contact with his psychic realities. If I employ a theory of causation and give

[1] The theory of causation is only valid in the domain of morality and only morality can *cause* anything. Meaning has no influence outside the psyche and causes nothing.

it expression in a circular argument[1] my transformation differs from that of the patient; his transformation falls in category C2 and mine in F3 and F4.

This account implies that the apparatus is secondary to the impulses that lie behind its employment—a conclusion which would not surprise a psycho-analyst. Nevertheless the apparatus matters. The impulses concerned determine (i) the way in which the apparatus is employed, and (ii) the fate of the apparatus itself. In severe disturbance it is possible to see apparatus employed in a manner calculated to destroy it. What, in a less disturbed patient, appears as a hostile attack on either the oedipal situation or a part-object oedipal situation, must, in the severely disturbed patient, be seen as an attack on the oedipal, or part-object oedipal, *pre-conception*—the apparatus that should make the relationship between the parents comprehensible and give it meaning. In disorders of thought interpretations must illuminate the condition of the apparatus of thinking, the nature of its deficiencies and the nature of the associated impulses. In practice I find I have constantly to give interpretations in the form that some impulse "leads to" a particular defect (or characteristic) of the mode of thought; or that some characteristic of the mode of thought "gives rise" to a particular impulse, as, for example, that frustration, engendered by failure to solve a problem, "leads to" a destructive attack on the analytic approach. I regard these statements as conversational formulations employing a theory I know to be false because it serves a useful purpose in the absence of the correct theory. This may, and often does, prove adequate in practice—it is usually adequate to speak in everyday life of sunrise. Nevertheless there are analytic situations, particularly when psychotic material is to the fore, when this is *not* adequate. The patient seems unable or unwilling to make for himself the adjustment of a conversational phrase which would make that phrase meaningful for him. The theory implicit in the interpretation must be exact. As I shall show later, this also applies to the emotional tone accompanying the interpretation: if

[1] For circular argument, see p. 111.

I am attempting to establish a K link, which is after all the case with any interpretation, there must be no emotion belonging to the H or L group. This may seem a commonplace of counter-transference theory, but it is not. A neurotic patient makes some allowance for human frailty; the psychotic patient either behaves as if the verbal communication had not been received, or, that it is a vehicle for transmission of some aspect of L or H—usually projection of it by the analyst into the patient.[1]

The patient's apparent demand for exactitude both with regard to the verbal communication itself and the emotional accompaniment seems to have some relationship to what I have said about the point "now". I spoke of this as associated with denudation of the elemental or primitive breast. In this context it is associated with inability to receive anything but a communication that is "pure".

Analysts are so accustomed to the fact that the link between analyst and patient is verbal that certain implications of this may escape scrutiny. These can be made to emerge more clearly by considering the verbal exchanges as transformations.

The analyst's transformations employ the vehicle of speech just as the musician's transformations are musical and the painter's pictorial. Though the analyst attempts to transform O, in accordance with the rules and discipline of verbal communication, this is not necessarily the case with the patient. He may, for example, transform O into what may *seem* to be a verbal communication but is to the analyst something akin to hallucination.[2] Such transformation (Tp β) belongs to the domain not of verbal communication but of hallucination, be it auditory, visual or tactile. It should therefore be helpful if, by analogy with painting, music or verbal communication, it were possible to understand the discipline and rules, so to speak, of hallucination.

[1] In successful analysis the patient brings to bear quite brilliant intuitive grasp of the possibilities that his analyst's deficiencies offer his super-ego for demolition of the analyst.

[2] What I say here is not exclusive of, but in addition to, what I have said about hallucination elsewhere.

The patient as receptor seems to receive everything as if it had the characteristics of the point, whether he is to understand time, or space, or meaning: as emitter he can only express transformations that are effected in a domain with the discipline of which we are unfamiliar. What "rules" govern the transformation of O into a visual hallucination rather than an auditory hallucination, or vice versa? or into hallucination rather than music or art or more ordinary forms of communication?

In discussion of transformation I drew attention to invariants; in painting there must be something that is invariant to the representation and that which is represented. It may be that the reaction stimulated is the element common to both object represented and representation. Yet one feels that something more is required than the reaction of the beholder—something present in object and its representation. If so, what is invariant in the word "cow" and the object it represents? If the word is onomatopoeic the sound can be regarded as invariant but such an element is relatively rare. It cannot satisfactorily be supposed that there is some simple factor like learning by heart that the name cow belongs to a particular animal. That memorization is present seems to be supported by incidents where an adult repeats to a child "Look, there is —— (whatever or whoever it is)!" when it reappears. If so, it may be part of being taught by communication of adult experience as opposed to learning from experience direct. It is easier to accept it as true that someone "cannot understand music" or "cannot understand painting" than to accept that a similar difficulty exists with regard to speech. Yet sometimes I think that this is so; the actual *medium* of speech is not understood.

The mother's inability to accept the projective identifications of the infant and the association of such failure with disturbances in understanding is matched by complications arising through the existence of an extremely understanding mother, particularly understanding by virtue of ability to *accept* projective identification. A reaction associated with this resembles character disorder, an unwillingness to face loss of an idyllic state for a new phase and suppression of the new phase because it involves pain. It is against this background of hallucinosis, projective identification, splitting and persecution, accepted as if it were the ideally happy state, that I want to consider the domain of verbal communication. The sense of well-being engendered by a belief in the existence of the perfectly understanding mother (or analyst) adds force to the fear and hatred of thoughts which are closely associated with, and may therefore be felt to be indistinguishable from, the "no-breast". A painful state of mind is clung to, including depression, because the alternative is felt to be worse, namely that thought and thinking mean that a near perfect breast has been destroyed.

The name, in its function of binding a constant conjunction, partakes of the nature of a definition; it commences by being significant, but meaningless, till experience gives it accumulations of meaning; it derives negative force both by virtue of its genesis as part of thought and by the necessary logic of its coming into existence precisely because the constant conjunction it binds is *not* any of the previous and already named constant conjunctions. Dislike of it is therefore derived from its genesis and from fear of the implications of its "use".[1] As naming and definition are inescapable this contributes to dislike of the unknown and the challenge it presents to the learner. The intensity of dislike depends on other factors. At what point the dislike of the unknown and its impact on the development of procedures which are a part of finding out must be regarded as pathological is an academic question; it is decided for the analyst whenever there is evidence of a desire to learn and an inability to do so. In such a situation primitive levels of thought are stimulated to discover the "cause" of the obstruction.[2] Evidence of the employment of a theory of causation is evidence of the operation of a theory that is not adequate. I shall consider the genesis of a theory of causation and its use with the aid of the grid and its two axes. Appearance

[1] Cf. Aristotle and definitions. *Topics*, VI, 4, 141b, 21.
[2] Cf. Hume, D.: *Enquiries Concerning Human Understanding*, Q 43–45. See also circular argument later, p. 111.

in a given situation—inquiry obstructed either by analyst or patient—must be assessed on the category in the grid to which it should be relegated. If it appears to belong to column 2 categories the presumption of a pathological origin will be strong. If it belongs to column 4 it is evidence, especially in a K link such as an analysis ought to be, for something compatible with healthy growth.

Ideally this inquiry should deal simultaneously with the process of transformation by which O is converted into thought, or whatever the alternatives to thought may be, and the processes of development (or transformation) which are associated with the *link* between thoughts and the *links* between the various alternatives to thought.

Invariant to β-elements and bizarre objects, in so far as they share the characteristics of β-elements, is the moral component of such objects. The moral component is inseparable from feelings of guilt and responsibility and from a sense that the *link* between one such object and another, and between these objects and the personality, is moral causation. The theory of causation, in a scientific sense in so far as it has one, is therefore an instance of carrying over from a moral domain an idea (for want of a better word) into a domain in which its original penumbra of moral association is inappropriate.[1]

The observation of constant conjunction of phenomena whose conjunction or coherence has not been previously observed, and therefore the whole process of Ps ↔ D interaction, definition and search for meaning that is to be attached to the conjunction, can be destroyed by the strength of a sense of causation and its moral implications. Patients show[2] that the resolution of a problem appears to present less difficulty if it can be regarded as belonging to a moral domain; causation, responsibility and therefore a controlling force (as opposed to helplessness) provide a framework within which omnipotence reigns. In certain

[1] Usurpation of ego-function by super-ego. See Chapter 4.

[2] And not only patients. The group is dominated by morality—I include of course the negative sense that shows as rebellion against morality—and this contributed to the atmosphere of hostility to individual thought on which Freud remarked.

circumstances, to be considered later,[1] the scene is thus set for conflict (reflected in controversies such as those on Science and Religion). This situation is portrayed in the Eden and Babel myths. The significance for the individual lies in its part in obstructing the Ps ↔ D interaction.

Hume's objection to a theory of causation supposes that since neither a hammer nor a nail can feel force it is not correct to speak of a nail being forced into position by the hammer, the term "force" being properly applicable only to the sense-experience of a human being who exerts force or on whom it is exerted. He supposes therefore that to speak of force as an external reality is a projection of human feeling. The fact that one merely follows the other is thus obscured. This argument does not satisfactorily dispose of an objective link between hammer and nail. To begin with, why is a selection made so that only the movement of the nail is considered and then only in relation to the hammer? There must be precedent "causes" that lead to the presence of nail and hammer. Furthermore it takes no account of the need of the human mind to apply a term, already with its penumbra of association and proper domain, in a different domain and because of its value as a model. For the analyst there is the added complication that, since he is dealing with beings like himself, there would appear to be justification for supposing that the relationship between two people was force if identification with one or other leads him to think that in such a situation he would feel force was being applied. The problem of conflict, which I shall name "Science versus Morals" as a prelude to finding meaning, will be found to be illuminated by the transformation of scientific thought into moral thought that is necessary for the former to be made suitable for action—column 6.

In spite of these objections I think Hume's argument has validity for psycho-analysis. In its extreme form it could mean that scientific validity was denied to a conjecture even though it was supported by common sense. (But the argument must not be supposed to be employed in an extreme form; if it is so employed it would be wise to consider why

---

[1] See below, p. 169.

the argument was employed in a manner that qualified it for column 2.) Hume's theory that an idea owes its genesis to a sense impression contrasts with the theory of force as the link between hammer and nail, for the latter is derived from an animistic outlook.

The earliest problems demanding solution are related to a link between two personalities. The breast, as analytic experience shows, can be regarded as an object with personality or as inanimate. Or it may be that no distinction between animate and inanimate is made. Sometimes a problem is "dealt with"[1] by regarding the object as a thing, sometimes by regarding it as if it were a person—an infant person. In either case O is being transformed; judgment of either operation must hinge on whether the solutions attempted are growth-producing or the reverse. If the solution is a pre-conception, and can be used in accordance with columns 3, 4, 5, it is growth-producing.

Patients can be observed to change their attitude to an object by changes in view-point[2] which may be perverse or analogous to changes of position that a surveyor, terrestrial or astronomical, uses to estimate the range of a distant object. The procedure involves splitting in time and space and, depending on the nature of the intention, may aid the solution of a problem by providing a substitute for "binocular vision" when "binocular vision" is not available, or hinder a solution by destroying "binocular vision"[3] when it is available.[4] The immediate relevance of this lies in the use of splitting as a method of achieving correlation. The mechanism involves bringing together the splits. The

---

[1] I use an ambiguous phrase deliberately.

[2] See discussion of vertices.

[3] See also circular argument, p. 111.

[4] Throughout this book I employ precisely the mechanism I attempt to describe as observable in analytic practice. To draw attention to these occasions at all frequently would burden the text with so many digressions that it would make a difficult subject appear more difficult. In this instance I am using a phrase taken from a domain of scientific statements appropriate to Optics and a high category of sophistication, row E or F, to provide a model which would be best classified as a member of row C. It is an example of the mechanism I am discussing as related to correlation. See also circular argument.

obstacle to correlation for a personality whose splitting is motivated by destructive impulses, is the need for two objects to be brought together creatively.

The instances examined in this chapter indicate that the mechanisms remain the same, but that the situation changes according to the emotional drives in operation—a banal enough conclusion, but its significance lies in what it may portend. I associated K with curiosity, but it is necessary to consider other impulses, emotions and instincts (I do not distinguish these terms because no distinction is precise enough) namely, the phenomena I have lumped together as L and H and the effect of the intrusion of one group on the other.

Hitherto I have considered the use of the grid almost entirely in terms of K and have not questioned its applicability to relationships with L and H dominant. To return to my "conclusion" that the character of a dynamic situation changes according to the emotional drives in operation even though the mechanisms are unaltered: I put the term "conclusion" in inverted commas because I am using it in a special way unrelated to any belief that some discussion has been "concluded". The statement made is a premise and is intended to fulfil the function of premises and postulates. That function I regard as marking a point of view[1] which is used as part of the mechanism of splitting and correlation to which I have referred.

This "view", which appears to ascribe a dominant position to emotion, is not a report, fact or discovery. In psycho-analysis there is difficulty in deciding when a statement is intended by its maker to represent a theory to be used if and when any realization appears to approximate to it (columns 4—n-1, n., of the grid), and when it is intended to be a statement of fact ("notation": grid 3). It is therefore often criticized in a way that would be appropriate to one belief but not to the other.

I shall combine the theory of dominance of emotion with the theory of transformation and use the grid to investigate both.[2]

[1] See vertices, Chapter 6.
[2] It would be more correct to say I shall correlate the three and see what eventuates from the correlation.

In Chapter 1, I used as a model of transformation the instance of the painting and its relationship to the object it purported to represent. I shall now use the image of reflection in water and the movement of air that disturbs it (Chapter 4). A representation, though distorted by emotion as a reflection in a lake might be distorted by a breeze, can be seen to have a relationship with the object. Equally, emotions that are active can be seen to have a relationship with the object even if disturbed by the representation. Again, the representation can be seen to be related to the emotions, and vice versa, even if disturbed by the object. To illustrate by clinical examples: a patient is dominated by hate of the analyst because of the transformation (Tp β) the analyst has undergone and the representation (Tp β) of the analyst that he now entertains. The patient entertains a representation (Tp β) of the analyst that is compatible with the hatred that has effected his transformation (Tp β). The patient entertains a transformation (Tp β) (it might be of a loved object) because of the hatred he feels for the person O of the analyst. It is inadequate to say there is a cause[1] for any of these situations. Yet I have said there is a relationship between the elements, and this means that one element effects and is effected by the others. Hume's argument that such a belief is a projection of an animistic outlook may not seem to apply to the view that one human being entertains of another. The fact that it is animistic may be obscured by the accident that the object observed is a human being. I shall suppose that the relationship is a "constant conjunction", that is to say, that the relationship is an element in the mind of the observer and may or may not have a counterpart in reality. I make no claim for objective reality, as far as I understand the meaning usually attributed to the term, but for me, a factual situation (conjectured) an emotional state (say hate, also conjectured) a representation (Tp β) are constantly conjoined and I record (grid E3) or bind (grid E1) it by the term "transformation".

It follows from the theory of transformations that whenever

[1] But see circular argument for the *value* of such a theory (p. 111).

I see one element of the equation O, Tp α, Tp β + L, or H or K, the others must be present. But I shall *not* assume that one causes the other, though for convenience I may (as I have already done when I used the phrase "because of the hatred", etc., p. 68) employ a theory of causation to express myself.[1] Indeed the object of binding what seems to be a constant conjunction of elements by a name "transformation" is in the hope of discovering the meaning of the constant conjunction.

The constant conjunction does not *have* to be marked by one word; it may be marked by two—e.g. "constant conjunction", or by a phrase, or an entire deductive system. Indeed such expansion may be an expression of the growth of meaning once the constant conjunction has been bound or recorded. (Columns 1 and 3.)

To return to the model of the reflection in water and its representation of transformation: in analysis all transformations, patient's or analyst's, are conventionally supposed to be expressed verbally. Such a supposition cannot legitimately be entertained with patients who transform in hallucinosis or some other unknown realm. The following problems may be discerned.

1. What is invariant to a name and the object named? For example, it appears that there is a flower rose (O) called "rose". What is it that leads a man who hears this word to relate it to a particular flower? What is invariant to the following marks on the paper—rose—and the flower visible in a garden?

2. Since I am proposing to classify statements, such as "rose", according to grid categories, and these statements are representations of transformations; since furthermore we know that a statement such as "I hate you" can be used in a manner compatible with column 1, or 6, or 2, and therefore represents a transformation whose elements are in a state of balance that differs according to whether it properly belongs to column 1 or 2 or 6, what difference does it make if the grid is being used to investigate an H link rather than K?

[1] I shall not draw attention to this, leaving the reader to note instances for himself, unless there is some especial reason for doing so, e.g. p. 68.

or L rather than H? The balance is different because the
components are different and to suppose that a change in
components makes no difference can only mean that in the
domain of the psyche the observer is incapable of discrimination and therefore of recognition of the selected fact that
gives coherence and meaning where none existed before.
Can the grid be used for situations other than K? And if
not, does this mean a defect in the grid or some basic
difference between L, H or K?

In analytic practice it is generally agreed that love or hate
between analyst and patient should not obtrude. Curiosity
cannot be banned if patient and analyst are to learn anything. It is a part of common experience that strong feelings
of love and hate affect ability to discriminate and learn.
Therefore it is worth considering what grid categories the
statements made by the two parties to an analysis, analyst
and patient, are when L or H obtrude in what should be a
K relationship. But the problem can also be regarded as
concerned with the appropriateness of the grid as an instrument to be used for investigating L or H links. Considering
the horizontal axis, there is no difficulty in retaining the
headings found useful for K because an L relationship
clearly cannot be regarded as excluding K either in logic or
reality. Therefore a statement expressing love might
perfectly well fall in column 1 as a definitory hypothesis.
But the question, in practice, is not simply whether a statement *can* fall in a particular category. There are two
questions involved. One is, whether I can formulate a theory
that a transformation associated with L, or suffused with
love, or perturbed by love, can be conceived of as falling in
categories of column 1. The other is, is a particular statement illuminated by being thought of as belonging to one
of the column 1 categories? The latter question is one that
must be answered through the analytic process. The former
must be answered with due consideration for methods of
theory-formation and the construction of instruments (such
as the grid) which are based on theoretical pre-conceptions.
Is the grid soundly constructed for use not only in K but
also for L and H links? If so, what is the difference between,

say, D$_1$ in K and D$_1$ in L? There must be a difference because it is hard to imagine a transformation, and all statements are transformations in the view I am putting forward, that is, affected by L being correctly placed, that is, placed in a manner that increases meaning, if it is placed in the same category as a transformation affected by K.

Though I am speaking of "transformations affected by . . ." and so implying causation, I do not wish the reader to infer my belief in the implied theory, except as a convenience in verbal communication. At this juncture a theory of causation is a hindrance to understanding the theory I wish to advance, namely, that any element in a transformation can appear to the analyst to affect any other element and vice versa. It appears to affect other elements in the transformation (on the analogy of atmospheric change, affecting the reflection) but other elements can be regarded, indifferently, as affecting L. Using the model to show its inadequacy to represent my meaning: the atmospheric change disturbs the reflection, but (it would be necessary to say), the disturbed reflection affects (or "causes") the atmospheric change. Such a theory would not commend itself as a useful theory about reflections in lakes but it is the theory of transformation that I wish to put forward. The transformation represents a constant conjunction and the idea that it has a cause, or that one element causes another I regard as derived from forces within the observer and not necessarily having a part in the conjunction observed. In short, the idea that the constant conjunction has a meaning may be logically (meaning psycho-logically) necessary but is not necessary to the constant conjunction. The importance of this for this discussion lies in the fact that L, H and K must be regarded as an essential element amongst all the elements seen to be constantly conjoined. This is true of the analyst's constant conjunctions and of those that he thinks are an aspect of the analysand's personality. Any transformation may thus be regarded as (*a*) an instance of the analyst's seeing a number of elements as constantly conjoined and therefore worth binding by the name "transformation", and (*b*) an instance of the analysand's seeing a number of elements as constantly conjoined and therefore to be bound by whatever name he regards as adequate. The interpretation given should then afford an opportunity for analyst and analysand to contrast two sets of transformation, the analyst's and the analysand's, and the analysand's and the analysand's (when the latter is affecting two transformations of the same O—which is commonly the case in conflict).

A common instance of the factors I am discussing can be seen in pictorial art where the picture (transformation) can be classified as a portrait, or a caricature, or a cartoon, and so on. O may be the same in all representations, but a different name is given according to the components of the transformation. In the named examples the dominance of L or H or K will influence classification of the whole.

I shall now consider "meaning" and "constant conjunction" in more detail, leaving discussion of L, H and K till later.

CHAPTER SIX

A CONSTANT conjunction is a function of consciousness in the observer. The observer feels that it is a necessity *for him* that the conjunction should have a meaning *for him*. Meaning is a function of self-love, self-hate or self-knowledge. It is not logically, but psycho-logically necessary. The constant conjunction, once named, must then be found, as a matter of psychic necessity, to have a meaning. Once psycho-logically necessary meaning has been achieved reason, as the slave of the passions, transforms psycho-logically necessary meaning into logically necessary meaning. Inadequacy of hallucinatory gratification to promote mental growth impels activity designed to provide "true" meaning: it is felt that the meaning attributed to the constant conjunction must have a counterpart in the realization of the conjunction. Therefore the activity of the reason as the slave of the passions is inadequate. In terms of the theory of pleasure/pain principle there is a conflict between pleasure principle and reality principle to obtain control of the reason. The objection to a meaningless universe (however big or small it may be thought to be) derives from fear that the lack of meaning is a sign that meaning has been destroyed and the threat this holds for essential narcissism. If any given universe cannot yield a meaning *for the individual*, his narcissism demands the existence of a god, or some ultimate object, for which it has a meaning from which meaning he is supposed to benefit. In some instances meaninglessness is attacked by splitting and projected into an object. Meaning or its lack, in analysis, is a function of self-love, self-hate, self-knowledge.

If narcissistic love is unsatisfied the development of love is disturbed and cannot extend to love of objects.

Disturbed self-love is accompanied by intolerance of meaning or its lack. The one contributes to the other. If the theories put forward in this book are felt to have or to lack meaning, they and the reasons for rejection, or acceptance, must be regarded as functions of L, H and K links of the self with the self.

The significance of self-love, -hate and -knowledge in psycho-analytic practice may be contrasted with its philo- sophical, moral or religious significance as it appears, to take one example, in the saying of Jesus that "No man hath greater love than this, that he lay down his life for another." Psycho-analysis is concerned with love as an aspect of mental development and the analyst must consider the maturity of love and "greatness" in relation to maturity.

The value of the vertical axis of the grid as marking steps in maturation or L or H could be supported from experience with patients. The analyst may ask himself which of his clinical experiences of L might appear to approximate to the category D4; and so with other categories.

Superficially an analytic session may appear boring, or featureless, alarming, or devoid of interest, good or bad. The analyst, seeing beyond the superficial, is aware that he is in the presence of intense emotion; there should be no occasion on which this is not apparent to him.

The intense experience is ineffable but once known cannot be mistaken; this chapter must be understood to relate to and be in preparation for participation in it for if such a contact is maintained the analyst can devote himself to evaluating and interpreting the central experience and, if he sees fit, the superficialities in which it is embedded.

One such group of superficialities pertains to the circum- stances in which analysis is conducted. These are usually physically comfortable and bear the stamp of unadventurous civilized existence. They therefore conspire against aware- ness that analysand and analyst are engaged on a venture which is as hazardous as activities in which the perils are more obvious and dramatic. In what the danger consists will depend on circumstances, but danger and awareness of danger are features of the situation with which the analyst should be in contact. The approach to it, to be effective, is "binocular"; the analyst must be aware, while attending to the patient's material, of the dangers of his association with that particular patient: he should also be able to see what the danger is that the patient is inviting him by his presence to share. I stress these points because what I have to say about the grid and transformations is incomprehensible without it.

An explorer's knowledge of instruments must be such that he can use them in situations of stress. The analyst must use instruments that are altered by the circumstances they are devised to study. The grid and the concept of transformations are altered by the situation they are devised to examine in proportion as they are brought to bear on it. They retain their character so long as they are employed *away* from the tense situation; after a session in which they have been employed, though so transformed by Ta α and by the tension of the session that the analyst may not be able to see that grid and transformation are in use, they resume the characteristics they possess extra-analytically. This is disquieting, but no one who tries to use the grid or transformation concepts in a session would doubt that it is true. Unless transformed so that the instrument (O = the grid) has become Ta β it loses power to illuminate during the session, but regains it afterwards. Untransformed, they would reduce the analyst to the state of a musician who, aware that the composition of which he was giving a concert performance was made up of scales and arpeggios, began to play it as if it were an exercise in scales and arpeggios.

No one can understand the grid or transformations without experience of their use as part of psycho-analytic practice.

Suppose that this essential contact is established and that the patient is making his contribution: the more it were possible to go into it the more complex would the contribution appear to be. If the analyst's attention is slanted to pick up the characteristics that determine grid classification it would be selective attention. Therefore construction of the grid is such that it picks up what is wanted for psycho-analysis.

Although home work is not done in an atmosphere of emotional tension, grid and transformation theory are applied to the recollection of such situations. The analyst's intuition, which it is the object of these reviews to exercise and develop, is operating in contact with the tense situation. It is important to distinguish between the grid (as it appears in my scheme) operating in tranquility on recollections, and the grid as part of the analyst's intuitive contact with the emotional situation itself.

The appearance in psycho-analysis of black-heads, spots, dots, staccato marks in musical scores, points, etc., can all be represented by the geometer's point; similarly the variety of supposedly phallic symbols can be represented by the geometer's line. I shall take advantage of this to demonstrate the difference of K and —K.

The point and the line, representing all Tp β's, are used by certain patients, who believe others do the same, as if they or their signs in painting, music, words, etc., were things. That is to say, such a patient hearing me say "point", or seeing a dot, behaves as if the point, however it is signified or represented, marks the place where the breast (or penis) was. Now this "place" seems to be invested by the patient with characteristics that less disturbed people might attribute to an object they would call a ghost. The point ($\cdot$) and the term "point" are taken as sensible manifestations of the "no-breast". In so far as I can express it in ordinary terms, the patient seems to think that the fact that the word "point" is used, is a sign of the presence of a non-existent breast, "the place where the breast was" having many of the characteristics of a breast that is hostile because it no longer exists. In short, the word "breast" is not recognized as a word representing a breast, but is thought to be the outward manifestation of a "no-breast", one of the characteristic qualities, so to speak, of the "no-breast" itself. It is in this way that a certain class of patient "concludes" that a thought is a thing, albeit a "thing" in a sense that a rational being does not ordinarily understand. Such a view contrasts with that which enables a mathematician to use a point, however represented, to elaborate a geometric system.

Similarly, it contrasts with the ordinary view of the word "breast" or "point" that enables it to be used to elaborate anatomical or physiological or artistic or aesthetic (in the philosophical sense) systems.

I can differentiate the views by regarding the extra-ordinary view as backward-looking and relating to what has been lost, and the ordinary view as forward-looking and relating to what can be found. Such a differentiation is not convenient because it implies a penumbra of associations, and therefore has implications, that limit my freedom of discussion. I shall therefore denote the extra-ordinary view by the sign $-K$ and the ordinary view by the sign K. I shall continue the process of differentiation of the ordinary from the extra-ordinary view by using as a model a system of co-ordinates, analogous to that employed by the algebraic geometer, in which two axes intersect at a point O. K will lie to the right of O, $-K$ to the left. I shall further suppose that O can be replaced by the point or the line or a word such as "breast" or "penis" or any other sign representing any constant conjunction. For this discussion I shall suppose the point replaces O as the origin. For the point to become adequate for manipulation in geometric systems it is clear that it should not be invested with a penumbra of inappropriate associations. Now the associations of a statement include feelings: indeed many of the associations of a verbal statement represent feelings. The objection to Aristotle's term for point, on the ground that it "meant" puncture and therefore was too closely tied to reality, may be matched by Aristotle's objection that Plato called the point the beginning of a line (*Metaph.* 992. a. 20). It suggests that the importance of a definition is to mark a constant conjunction without the evocation of feelings; but something seems real only when there are feelings about it. The negative quality of a definition, then, relates to the need to exclude existing emotion as well as ideas. If "point" is to be available for use in K it must be defined to exclude the penumbra of associations with which it is invested; it has to be developed so that it reaches the stage represented by D category. The realization which will approximate to it will be an emotional experience. It must lend itself to saturation by an emotional experience and its sign should represent this.

As I do not attempt clinical description except by way of illustration I shall very briefly sketch the development in K of the geometrical elaboration. The sketch represents clinical experience and is accurate as far as only one experience can be.

The geometrical elaboration proceeds as follows: commencing with a point, line or any more complex figure such as those associated with the theorem of Pythagoras, the proposition is read off the figure, that is to say, it seems to be regarded as self-evident from the nature of the figure. Inspection of the figure may be followed by a formulation in terms other than pictorial. Plutarch gives a fanciful and oedipal description[1] of the 3, 4, 5 triangle. The mathematical development may have been achieved by transformation of the visual image into an arithmetical formulation. However that may be, my analytical experience is compatible with a development that proceeds from the *complete* visual image to elaboration in non-visual terms; that is from row C categories to row H, though I did not witness a row H transformation. I have no evidence for mathematical formulations that are not geometric in origin (other than material suggesting a relationship between having a third son and having three sons). What is not clear is the reason for a geometric rather than verbal development.

As I have no evidence in my experience, with one possible exception, of mathematical change in −K I shall confine myself to verbal transformations.

The point has appeared clinically as dot or dots, spot or spots ("spots" in or before the eyes is a fairly common phenomenon). I have described the point or line as an object indistinguishable from the place where the breast or penis was. Owing to the difficulty of being sure what the patient is experiencing I resort to a variety of descriptions, each of which is unsatisfactory. The spot, for example, seems to be part conscience, part breast, part faeces, destroyed, non-existent yet present, cruel and malignant. The inadequacy of description or categorization as thought at all has led me to the term β-element as a method of representing it. The spoken word seems significant only because it is invisible and intangible; the visual image is similarly

---

[1] Quoted by Heath: *The Thirteen Books of Euclid's Elements*, vol. 1, p. 417.

significant because it is inaudible. Every word represents what is not—a "no-thing", to be distinguished from "nothing".

The patient's attention passes from one β-element to the next, all linked by a chain of pseudo-causation to deny that their "cause" or genesis lay in the destruction and dispersal of their common origin. Such manifestations are compatible with Melanie Klein's theory of splitting and projective identification which she elaborated to describe aspects of the infant's relationship with the breast. The aspect that is most relevant to discussion of K and −K is the breast's association with provision of meaning. It will be remembered that a fear that it is dying is, in accordance with Melanie Klein's theory, projected into the mother's breast. It should be taken back purged of its painful quality and invested with more benign associations, but as I said in my paper on thinking[1] it may in some circumstances be denuded of such meaning as it has, so that the transaction terminates in the infant dominated by a re-introjected nameless dread.

I recall this to explain the behaviour of the patient who strives to link in a chain of pseudo-causation a number of visual images (or other elements) in the way described.[2] In K and −K the analyst and analysand are searching for meaning. The column 4 categories, which I have described as corresponding to Freud's term "attention" are searching for meaning. Any element categorized by the column 4 use is therefore being employed to discover meaning. (Contrasted with 3, notation, which is concerned with retaining meaning and 5, which may now be further differentiated from 4 as being concerned with the search for *moral* meaning.)

Pseudo-causation is the −K version of causation (which falls in the K domain). Both pseudo-causation and causation are "linear" in character. That is, the elements in a chain of causation may be represented geometrically by points in a line. The idea of causation is itself an assertion (in grid terms it falls in one of the categories of column 1) that certain elements are constantly conjoined and that the conjunction

---

[1] Bion, W. R.: *A Theory of Thinking*, 1961.
[2] See Chapter 4.

is one of cause and effect. It is therefore an assertion that the conjunction has a meaning.

Both representations may be compared with $P \leftrightarrow D$ and selected fact.

Suppose we regard the linear representation, as it occurs in K and —K, in the light of the theory of transformations: the line of points in —K may then be regarded as a version of the straight line of points in K. Furthermore, we may consider the line in —K as a disturbed version of the straight line in K, or vice versa. What then is the disturbance?

From the psycho-analytical point of view the most likely source of disturbance can be regarded as emotional. This source can be further regarded as lying in the individual's (*a*) narcissism and (*b*) social-ism. In so far as the geometrical representation can be regarded as a visual image it can be related to the model[1] of the reflection of objects in a disturbed surface such as a sheet of water. The reflecting surface and the source of the disturbance would both represent parts of the personality.

Narcissism and social-ism may be regarded as at opposite poles; I shall not consider what they are poles of but shall suppose that the intensity of narcissism falls off as the intensity of social-ism increases, and vice versa. Further, I shall suppose that the increase of intensity in narcissism is accompanied by a narrowing or concentration of emotion till it can be said to be one emotion such as love or hate or fear or sex or any other. Similarly the intensity of social-ism is accompanied by a widening of the spectrum of emotions. I shall further suppose that the total range from intense narcissism to intense social-ism is subject to splitting. In other words, that there can be a state in which intense narcissistic hate is split off from all other feelings and that this is true of all feelings in turn. The same description will apply to splitting of the social feelings.

Splitting need not be associated with L or H. It may be a function of K in which case it is what is scientifically known as analysis and is quite commonly used in psycho-analysis. If the range narcissism $\leftrightarrow$ social-ism is regarded as split, for

---

[1] See Chapter 4.

whatever reason, it may be represented geometrically by points on a line. As we shall have later to consider the geometrical representation of certain states by control (from a point) and parallel projection (from a series of points) and the transformations and invariants associated with them, splitting of the range narcissism ↔ social-ism is important.

The importance for the psycho-analyst of the range narcissism ↔ social-ism can be grasped by considering the close relationship of meaning and narcissism.[1]

The infant's experience of the breast as the source of emotional experiences (later represented by terms such as love, understanding, meaning) means that disturbances in relationship with the breast involve disturbance over a wide range of adult relationships. The function of the breast in supplying meaning is important for the development of a capacity to learn. In an extreme instance, namely the fear of the total destruction of the breast, not only does this involve fears that he has ceased to exist (since without the breast he is not viable) but fears that meaning itself, as if it were matter, had ceased to exist. In some contingencies the breast is not regarded as the source of meaning so much as meaning itself. This anxiety is often screened by the fact that the analyst gives interpretations and thus seems to provide evidence that meaning exists. If this is not observed the patient's intolerance of meaninglessness is not interpreted: he will pour out a flood of words so that he can evoke a response indicating that meaning exists either in his own behaviour or in that of the analyst. Since the first requisite for the discovery of the meaning of any conjunction depends on the ability to admit that the phenomena may have no meaning, an inability to admit that they have no meaning stifles the possibility of curiosity at the outset. The same is true of love and hate. The need to manipulate the session to evoke evidence of the existence of meaning extends to a need to evoke evidence of the existence of love and hate. Anyone with experience of the psychotic personality will be familiar with the probing, incessantly active, designed to tap sources of counter-transference. The patient's associations

[1] See Chapter 6.

are directed to obtaining evidence of meaning and emotion (here broadly divided into two all-embracing categories of love and hate). Since the patient's attention is directed to finding evidence of meaning, but not to finding what the meaning is, interpretations have little effect in producing change until the patient sees that he is tapping a source of reassurance to provide an *antidote* to his problem and not a *solution* of it.

The thought, represented by a word or other sign, may, when it is significant as a no-thing, be represented by a point ($\cdot$). The point may then represent the position where the breast was, or may even *be* the no-breast. The same is true of the line, whether it is represented by the word line or a mark made on the ground or on paper. The circle, useful to some personalities as a visual image of "inside and outside", is to other personalities, notably the psychotic, evidence that no such dividing membrane exists.

Intolerance of a no-thing, taken together with the conviction that any object capable of a representative function is, by virtue of what the sane personality regards as its representative function, not a representation at all but a no-thing itself, precludes the possibility of words, circles, points and lines being used in the furtherance of learning from experience. They become a provocation to substitute the thing for the no-thing, and the thing itself as an instrument to take the place of representations when representations are a necessity as they are in the realm of thinking. Thus actual murder is to be sought instead of the thought represented by the word "murder", an actual breast or penis rather than the thought represented by those words, and so on until quite complex actions and real objects are elaborated as part of acting-out. Such procedures do not produce the results ordinarily achieved by thought, but contribute to states approximating to stupor, fear of stupor, hallucinosis, fear of hallucinosis, megalomania and fear of megalomania.[1]

I now explore some implications of the concurrence of elements of verbal with elements of geometrical formulation.

[1] See Chapter 12.

The association of the circle with "in and out" contributes to the difficulty of understanding the concepts of the line that cuts a circle in points that are conjugate complex. The difficulty arises from the supposition that the line that does so lies "outside" the circle; as opposed to the line that cuts it in two points, whose roots are real and distinct, and is supposed to lie "inside" the circle. The difficulty is diminished if there is no intolerance of the no-thing to contend with and therefore no opposition to a term of which the meaning is undetermined.

The simple example I have taken of the straight line that may cut a circle in two points that are (i) real and distinct, or, (ii) real and coincident (if the line is a tangent), or (iii) conjugate complex (if the line lies entirely "outside the circle") poses a problem that the mathematician has been able to solve by taking a mathematical point of view, but I use it to illustrate the nature of the psychological problem. I shall state this as follows: in the domain of thought where a straight line can be regarded as lying within, or touching, or wholly outside, a circle, a transformation has been effected whereby certain characteristics, lending themselves to mathematical manipulation, have been manipulated mathematically to adumbrate and then solve a mathematical problem. The residual characteristics however retain their problem, un-named (un-bound) and so uninvestigated. Hallucinosis is a domain, analogous to that of mathematics, in which their solution is sought. The mathematical problem resembles a psycho-analytic problem in that it is necessary that the solution should have a wide degree of applicability and acceptance and so avoid the need to apply different arguments to different cases when the different cases appear to have essentially the same configuration. Any analyst will recognize the confusion that is caused, or at best the sense of dissatisfaction that prevails, when a discussion by members makes it quite clear that the configuration of the case is apprehended by all, but the arguments formulated in its elucidation vary from member to member and from case to case. It is essential that such a state of affairs should be made unnecessary if progress is to take place. The search must be for formulations that represent the essential similarity of the configurations, recognized by all who deal with them, and thus to make unnecessary the *ad hoc* nature of so many psycho-analytic theories.

The individual error can always be recognized and allowed for if once the lack of a unifying theory, applicable to all similar configurations, has been recognized and eliminated. It will be noted that in writing of "similar configurations" I am pre-supposing the presence of invariants which are consciously or unconsciously recognized as such.

The geometric problem may appear more intractable than it need be by the apparatus of circles and straight lines drawn on paper. Included in this apparatus and of paramount importance, for the paper representations are not necessary, is the mental equipment of concepts such as inside and outside and the rules for their manipulation. Ignoring for the present any question of psycho-pathological inhibitions, it is evident that the inadequate apparatus must be replaced by a better. If we place ourselves in the position of the mathematician before Cartesian co-ordinates had been invented and before the geometric approach could be transformed into an algebraic approach (or in the position of the therapist before psycho-analysis was discovered or invented), it is easy to suppose that our dilemma would be the result of inadequate knowledge and experience, or simply lack of mental acuity. Such an explanation, however convincingly supported by the facts, is open to the objection that is levelled against the state of affairs where a number of different arguments are educed to apply to what appear to be different cases of the same configuration. For I have in this present argument proposed ignoring the presence of psychopathological inhibitions, and it is evident that such an exclusion makes any theory based on it exclude the similarity of the configuration in the two cases: in one, of the person unable to tolerate the no-thing, and in the other, the person who lacks the knowledge of Cartesian co-ordinates and algebraic manipulation. I propose therefore to suppose that the personality who cannot tolerate the point (breast, penis, and other verbal representations) and the pre-Cartesian mathematician (the prefix, pre- being used not in a social-temporal sense but as a term for a stage in individual development) to be in the same predicament. This I shall do by assuming that the mathematician is unconscious of the system of co-ordinates or algebraic manipulation.

By this means the two personalities can be differentiated by reference to the same frame. This disturbed patient can be said to be conscious of a "past" that no longer exists and the mathematician to be unconscious of a "future" that has not come to pass.

I now transform the theory adumbrated in the preceding paragraph to the domain of the mind; in doing so, the temporal component is first transformed into a scale at one end of which is the past and at the other the future. This description is inadequate as I wish to divest the concept of its associations of time and space. I shall do this by giving the term unconscious a sense, thus: $\overrightarrow{\text{unconscious}}$ and $\overleftarrow{\text{unconscious}}$; reciprocally, $\overrightarrow{\text{conscious}}$ and $\overleftarrow{\text{conscious}}$. The state of mind of the mathematician unaware of mathematical formal artifices can then be represented by $\overrightarrow{\text{unconscious}}$ and that of the disturbed patient by $\overleftarrow{\text{conscious}}$.

It will be seen that as it stands the last statement is ambiguous for it can be taken to represent a passive statement that the patient knows of his past as any ordinary personality might do. In fact it must represent an active hallucinatory state in which he is conscious of being in a past that replaces and excludes the present. Similarly $\overrightarrow{\text{conscious}}$ does not represent an awareness that events of some sort will take place in the future: it represents a replacement and exclusion of the present by a hallucinatory state of gratification either of foreboding or of pleasurable anticipation. An instance would be a patient who was conscious of unknown (because nothing has taken place) dread in a state of perpetual imminence or reciprocally of $\overleftarrow{\text{unknown}}$ pleasure equally imminent. The tone of conscious

$\xrightarrow{\hspace{1.5cm}}$
and conscious is determined by factors I am not at present
$\xleftarrow{\hspace{1cm}}$ $\xrightarrow{\hspace{1.5cm}}$
discussing. Unconscious and unconscious will be marked by
the presence of elements belonging to column 2 categories.
Typical of this would be theories about the past or future
that are known to be false. If it is correct to assume that
$\xleftarrow{\hspace{2cm}}$
column 2 categories are related to unconscious and
$\xrightarrow{\hspace{1.5cm}}$
unconscious we must consider what relationship exists
$\xleftarrow{\hspace{1.2cm}}$ $\xrightarrow{\hspace{1.5cm}}$
between column 4 categories and conscious and conscious
for it is natural to suppose there is a relationship between
attention to a problem and *consciousness* of it. If it is to be
assumed that this is true of a problem it is legitimate to
assume it is also true of a state of pleasure or unpleasure. It
can now be seen that conscious and unconscious, with a sign
for sense, are signs for something that is a denial of "the
present" and can accordingly represent the Kleinian theory
of splitting and projective identification. The realization
represented by these theories and signs, annihilated time,
can be visualized as a point—"where the present used to be".

By definition the term conscious relates to states within the
personality; consciousness of an external reality is secondary
to consciousness of an internal psychic reality. Indeed
consciousness of an external reality depends on the person's
ability to tolerate being reminded of an internal reality.[1] If
he cannot tolerate being reminded of an internal reality it
may involve widespread employment of column 2 categories
to keep awareness of aspects of real external objects at bay.

Before proceeding further, the reader may find it helpful
to reconsider any difficulties he has in understanding formulations involving differences in point-pairs. If he has
difficulty in understanding points that are conjugate complex,
real and coincident, real and distinct, he can compare this
experience of difficulty with the difficulty he may feel in
understanding the following problem:

Two breasts have disappeared. Or perhaps it would be

[1] Relationship between the external and internal reality is thus similar to
the relationship between pre-conception and the realization approximating to
it. It is reminiscent of Plato's theory of Forms.

more accurate to say they have shrunk or faded away until only two points remain. The protagonist may feel reconciled to this fact or he may feel quite unable to tolerate these spots (or points or (·)) as to him they are either places where the breasts were, or, more poignantly, no-breasts. As he watches they appear to come together until they are coincident with each other and the boundary of his personality. They might just as well have travelled towards each other in a straight line and so coincided without touching him. But suppose they have travelled towards, or been drawn towards, him at the same time: then the line along which they travel to meet each other has been pulled into a curve that touches his personality at the point of coincidence. Then they disappear. Where have they gone? If he had an inside or an outside they might have gone inside him or gone out the other side. But suppose they are not inside or outside. Worse still, suppose there is no inside or outside, that he himself is only a place-where-he-used-to-be, a place-where-inside-and-outside-used-to-be?

The elements of the problem are: (i) the no-breast, or point, or (·), (ii) the no-penis, or straight line or (———), and (iii) the no-inside-or-outside, or circle or ($\bigcirc$).

We can now allow our lack of understanding to impel curiosity along paths that are apparently different. Starting, say, at the no-inside-or-outside, we may proceed towards sophistication by one of two paths, which lead respectively to the concept of a circle in one instance (the geometer's view) and in the other to the concept of depersonalization.

Or, we may proceed by using both paths; before this I shall discuss some problems of the no-penis, straight line, (———).

It will be noticed that some configurations in which the no-breast and no-penis are involved suggest the possibility that it is unnecessary to have two concepts, of straight line and point, and that they could be replaced by a single concept.

The pre-Euclidean definition of a straight line, given by Plato, seems to depend on a visual impression of a straight line as it would appear to an eye placed at one end. The

geometer's need to make the definition independent
of an implied appeal to vision can be expressed in grid
terms as a process of transformation from C_1–H_1. I shall
use the sign to imply sense from $\uparrow$ for H to A, and for
$\downarrow$ A to H.

I shall commence my investigation of the point and line
as visual images. As I propose first to explore their characteristics as "no-things" the sense will be towards β-elements.
Therefore the trend of the investigation of the point and line
can be indicated by writing the category of the objects
concerned as $C_1 \uparrow$. When I wish to indicate that I am
reversing the trend I shall write the category of the object
with the appropriate sign.

Reversing the procedure of the geometer, who needs to
divest the straight line C_1 of its visual implications and does
so by resort to algebraic calculi H_1, we progress $H_1 \uparrow$,
$C_1 \uparrow$ to A_1.

The category A_1 indicates that the straight line is a
thought that is indistinguishable from a thing and is related
to the β-elements as I have at various times described them.
In view of the preceding discussion we may describe the
straight line of category A_1 as being, indifferently, a no-
thing, a no-thought (in so far as it is a "thing"), a no-penis;
in short, many descriptive expansions may be applied to it,
but all will be characterized by the vice attributed to
fundamental definitions of geometry, namely, that all are
negative.

I have previously given my reasons for supporting the
definition of a definition as something negative *in essence*; a
definition should implicitly or explicitly be a statement that
the statement itself is not any *past* statement (if not, where
would be the need for the statement?) and has no meaning
(if it had there would be no need for a definition) to bind
the constantly conjoined elements; for they are to be bound
so that their meaning can be determined. It is therefore
quite appropriate that we should arrive by way of discussion
of the no-thing at characteristics which are impregnated
with a quality regarded by the scientist (proceeding in
thought to $H_1 \downarrow$) as undesirable.

To return to the straight line. Suppose we approach it as it is in category C1. As a visual image we can subject it to a number of manipulations that are excluded by the rules that govern its manipulation as an H1 object. Any mathematical terms I employ must be considered likewise to be freed from the rigour that governs the regulation of H1 elements when they are H1 elements themselves.

We may start with a mental image of a line in front of us. We can suppose that the two ends of the line are joined to our eye or that our eye projects the line outwards to a point where we want it. In both instances the eye is the vertex of a configuration of lines. We can rotate the line so that it is end-on to our "line of sight" and so appears as a point. Or we may consider that the point is projected outward while remaining attached to the eye. If projected outwards while remaining attached it becomes stretched out and can be considered therefore as a line. The line "seen" end-on and the point stretched out may be regarded as duals, or, the same object transformed under projection and possessing a different sense according to whether it is supposed to be proceeding from the eye or drawn in to it. I have already discussed other manipulations of these visual images and shall not therefore elaborate further; the reader can continue the exercise for himself. The immediate question is whether it is helpful to consider point or line as separate entities or whether it is better to consider them as different manifestations of one entity. But this raises the immediate question, better or useful to whom and for what? So long as I concern myself with visual images there seems to be freedom. If I want to use the point to enclose an object I can make it stretch out so that it catches up with its tail, the object to be enclosed lying inside the circle described. But is this a point with a tail, or a circle?

Suppose for the purposes of discussion it is convenient to replace point and line by a single object. This involves simplification in that we now have one object for all configurations but it involves restriction to objects of category C1 and resort to projection from a vertex.

Suppose the problem chosen (enclosure) proves recalci-trant[1]; we may vary the choice of vertex spatially, or from one sense to another, say visual to auditory. The no-thing owes its existence to the alimentary system as a model of the mind in its function of employing thought. Assuming the visual mental system, despite its freedom, is inadequate to provide a solution to problems of enclosure, is it possible to find some shift of vertex that will neutralize the obstacles encountered in employing the eye as a vertex of the mental visual system? There is nothing out of the way in making such an approach; as we saw, conversational English betrays the widespread use of alimentary metaphor when processes of thought are in dispute.[2] Equally common are locutions such as being "hot on the scent" of a problem, "smelling a rat", etc., but change to a vertex provided by the mental counterpart of a sense of smell, so poorly endowed verbally, simplifies the problem of enclosure, thanks to ideas of inspiration and expiration, but complicates all else further.

To shift from a vertex of one "sense" or "system" to another affords a way out of a difficulty that use of one vertex alone makes impossible. Apart from the problem of transformation of olfactory, or respiratory, representation into verbal representation the respiratory mental counterpart is no less effective than the visual in accepting point and line. The use of an aural mental counterpart to provide another vertex reveals some interesting comparisons with the alimentary, visual and respiratory vertices. Noise presents problems that sound, treated musically, can transcend. Musical methods of notation are in their adequacy reminis-cent of algebraic methods of geometrical notation. But the important and striking feature revealed by a comparison of the mental counterparts of visual with other vertices is the superior power of the visual vertex to illuminate (I find I turn spontaneously to the use of verbal representations of visual elements to express my meaning) a problem over that of all other mental counterparts of the senses. Reversal of

---

[1] As it well may—even to the infant.
[2] See Bion, W. R.: *Learning from Experience.* Chapter 3.

direction in the system of which the vertex is a part is
associated with what are ordinarily known as hallucinations.
The supremacy of the visual vertex contributes to my belief
that the solution of the problem of communicating psycho-
analytically will have to be found through row C elements
to geometrical formulation and thence to row H elements.

Before leaving the discussion of choice of vertices I shall
consider the vertex provided by the mental counterpart of
the reproductory system. First I deal with a matter that may
have puzzled the reader, namely my use of the term "mental
counterpart".

If the reader visualizes a point or a line, without representation of it on paper, he does something that has been
variously described as "using his inward eye", "visualizing",
"seeing in imagination", etc. I consider this activity to
depend on a "mental counterpart of the sense of sight".
Similarly the "bitterness" of a memory is dependent on a
mental counterpart of the alimentary system; similarly with
others including the reproductory system.

The "inner" reproductory system, as I may call the mental
counterpart of the reproductory system by analogy with the
"inward eye" of the mental counterpart of the visual system,
must not be confused with awareness of reproductive activity
any more than visual images that are related to the activity
of the mental counterpart of sight are to be confused with
objects of sight. The mental counterpart of the reproductory
system is related to premonitions of pleasure and pain. The
second source of confusion may lie in my use of the term
vertex. I am unwilling to use a term such as "point-of-view"
because I do not wish to be reduced to writing "from the
point of view of digestion", or "from the point of view of a
sense of smell" when the distinctions between metaphorical
and literal usages are fine yet difficult to preserve. I can
describe my use of the term "vertex" as an example of
taking a mathematical term, (grid category H1) and using
it as a model (grid category C1). With the reproductory
mental counterpart as vertex, transformation of the point or
line is into a surface or plane. In the last sentence I resort
to verbal representation of geometrical visual images. This

occurs so naturally as to suggest that the visual mental counterpart has supremacy over other mental counterparts; visual images lend themselves to transformation in different media. In using the term "vertex" I employ a geometrical concept of a high degree of sophistication, but as used by me its grid category is C_1.

To sum up: The point/line may be transformed by central projection from any one of a number of vertices, or it may be transformed by parallel projection by a single point at infinity. What this may mean must be discussed below, together with the use of the point to mark a vertex of projection.

CHAPTER SEVEN

THE "point" and the "line" represent visual images which remain invariant under a wide range of conditions. The same is true of the visual images associated with the propositions of Euclid; hence the propositions themselves are communicated over long periods of time and between widely separated cultures and races. This may appear to be true of any visual representation, such as cave paintings, but although the column 3 component, record or notation, is strong, the artistic representation does not appear to be so rich in ideational content as the geometrical representation is. The geometer Bhāskara (b. A.D. 1114) drew four right-angled triangles inwards one on each side of the square of the hypotenuse and left it with the comment "See!"[1] There are two dissimilar observations that can be made. One is mathematical and can be stated: $C^2 = 4\dfrac{ab}{2} + (a - b)^2 = a^2 - b^2$; the other is mythical and can be stated: of the 3, 4, 5, triangle 3 is the first odd number and is perfect, 4 is the square on an even side 2, while 5 partly resembles the father and partly the mother, being the sum of 3 and 2, "and we must then liken the perpendicular to the male, the base to the female and the hypotenuse to the offspring of both".

The mathematical statement of the theme has been profitable and has led to development. The mythological statement, though widely spread, has not. Is it possible to release it from its fetters by reverting to point and line?

If we use the point alone to construct a square we can produce the following effects:

1	2	3	4	5

[1] Heath, T.: *The Thirteen Books of Euclid's Elements.*

In each case we have added a gnomon to the previous figure. It could represent accumulative if not creative activity. It adds to something or someone not specified. Whether we regard it as creative or not depends on whether ↑ ↓ represent its direction and a process of coherence or disintegration. If the direction is ↑ the trend is destruction of the capacity for thought. In verbal terms, if the process is from square to fragmentation of the square[1] it can be distinguished from the process of integrating fragments to make a square by calling the former creative, the latter destructive. If the horizontal axis represents uses there should be some relatedness between the elements of one column to the preceding and subsequent column, such as I have established between rows and put forward tentatively for the columns. It is easy to see that such a relationship might exist between 1, 3, 4, and 5 in that the order may be seen as one of increasing curiosity, at least in K, and possibly in L and H also. But 2 does not fit into such a progression. It might be better to replace it by a sign ← indicating that the element so distinguished was a use of that particular element to suppress another. $\overleftarrow{3}$ would then indicate the element was being employed to note or record something with the express purpose of exclusion of a true statement. But the antithesis I require is to a use in its fundamental nature. The $\overleftarrow{\text{square}}$ should mean the total denial of any initiative that $\overrightarrow{\text{square}}$ could effect. $\overrightarrow{3}$ would mean notation that is growth-producing: $\overleftarrow{3}$ would mean notation that was growth-inhibiting. But in fact I want to give the ← the quality of binding or definition as I have described it and that being so it must be understood to have no meaning that exists already.

What meaning can be attributed to $\overleftarrow{1-n}$? It is *not* that 4 is transformed into 3, unless we suppose that curiosity, once aroused so that column 3 elements become column 4 elements, might again subside so that column 4 elements

[1] The points can be so disposed that their number represents a square but their visual impression does not: which "view" (vertex) are we to adopt?

left a residue of column 3 elements. This change is better represented by denoting the terminal categories thus: $3 \leftarrow 4$. If we assume that the progression of uses is not linear there is no difficulty in writing $n \rightarrow 2$ or $2 \leftarrow n$ without assuming any transition from column 5 to 4 to 3 to 2. Suppose $3 \rightarrow 4$ accompanied by suspicion. Suppose 4 leads to stimulation of impotent envy and hate. Destructive retreat takes place $4 \rightarrow 1$. The fragmentation of point and line cannot go beyond the point; though the line may be annihilated, having been transformed into a series of points, to a single point, to the place where the point was, this last is still a point. The point is thus indestructible. A patient's state of mind could be represented by such a model on occasions when he continues attack after attack on objects by which he is persecuted.

Such behaviour is determined more by the strength[1] of emotions than by their character. A desire to be loving and creative turns to hate and destructiveness if it is frustrated by disparity between equipment and ambition. This is true of every impulse to act, including impulses to change from one state of mind to another. Such an impulse is analogous to the impulse to translate thought into action.

It sometimes helps to illuminate an analytic problem by speaking of a characteristic as appearing to the patient a "ghost of the past". The infant experiences what may be called ghosts of the future. Such locutions are possible to adult investigations for maturity provides terms born of experience together with facility in their manipulation. But the facts of personality, its own and that of others, exist for the infant and present him with problems that he must solve. Is there some adult problem that will provide an analogy for what the infant appears to experience? What analogy is available to the infant by aid of which it can approach its problems of personality? What past problems provide us with analogies for our present problems? What in our present problems is analogous to problems we have encountered in the past?

The problem of the personality at the crossroads, the

[1] See Hyperbole.

problem of what impulses must dominate when thought is translated into action,[1] or from meditation into decision, or from one state of mind into another, may be regarded as one of power and the seizure of a commanding position. This struggle may be regarded indifferently as taking place within the psyche, outside it, or tangentially; the model may be that of Oedipus at the crossroads at Thebes or the circle whose circumference is intersected at two actual and separate points, two points that are actual and coincident or two that are conjugate and complex.

The advantage of using the Oedipus myth to represent the row C category version is economy and avoidance of a whole series of *ad hoc* models and theories for different problems that have the same configurations. The circle cut by the line offers a connection with point and line and a model for inside and outside. Later we shall have to consider the appropriateness or relevance of inside and outside to emotional states recognized to be "infectious" or "contagious".

Emergence of a group of impulses as dominant in the psyche involves conflict within the personality and crisis outside but this same crisis can be seen as the point at which $T\alpha$ gives rise to $T\beta$.

A proper use of the oedipal elements is obstructed by a tendency to allow the narrative form of the myth to impose a cause-and-effect outlook on the investigator. The theory of causation is implied in and inseparable from the narrative form of the myth, but the narrative form is a function of column 3 categories and is related directly to notation. The confusion of notation, particularly in its association with narrative and a theory of causation, with categories of columns 4 and 5, attention and investigation, obscures the importance in learning from experience of the mechanism of $Ps \leftrightarrow D$. The essential of the narrative form is that it permits of an easy memorization, as one might memorize a mathematical formula, of a constant conjunction. The narrative form, with its implication of causation, is relevant and significant to the myth's function to record a constant

[1] See Transformation: super-ego vertex and ego vertex.

conjunction, but the relationship in which the constantly conjoined elements are combined depends on the relationship of the conjunction to Transformation. I shall therefore reconsider Transformation.[1]

Transformation may be a transference of characteristics from one situation to another, from one medium to another, a rigid motion, or a projective transformation. A musician or artist may transfer or project an emotional experience through $T \alpha$ to the finished product, $T \beta$, which may be a musical composition or a painting. If the transformation is considered to extend to the state of mind of the artist's public the emotional experience O may be regarded as transformed into the same medium—another emotional experience.

If the transformation is in the same medium one man's state of mind serves to produce, not *any* state of mind in another man, but a *particular* state of mind in which the invariants are such that $T \beta$, in the second man, can be seen to relate to T, the first man's emotional response to O.

The transformation cannot occur without an emotional experience such that its proper model is the scene of violence at the crossroads at Thebes. Stating the model in other terms, the elements that must be formulated to establish their relation to each other are: the no-penis (one that is yet to be) with the no-penis (where the penis used to be).

Narrative and cause-and-effect are intrinsic to notation or record. The story of the meeting at Thebes crossroads belongs to category C_3. Is there any essential difference between the record C_3 and the signification of constant conjunction by C_1 (definitory hypotheses)? A term "cat" (C_1) signifies a constant conjunction. So does the crossroads episode I have placed in C_3. There is no narrative and no causation theory in "cat". The crossroads narrative has power to represent murderous feeling as part of the constant conjunction. C_1 differs from C_3 in that the crossroads narrative, if placed correctly in C_1, would indicate the

---

[1] The narrative, by introducing cause and effect as a means of binding *its* elements, *mis*-represents the constant conjunction relationship. Cause and effect is proper to the *narrative* but has no corresponding link between one element and another in the realization. In the realization the elements are merely conjoined.

boundary within which the problem was to be completed. C3 would indicate that the story represented an element, part of a record, of a problem stated but incompletely. H1 would be a category in which only those elements would find a place which implied closure, e.g. the primitive counterparts of a circle cut by a line in two points, actual and separate. H3, however, would require that there was no limiting boundary. If the category of the episode were H3 it would represent an emotional experience outside the personality but cutting it at two points quite different from the point pair of H1. Alternatively, the two straight lines, representing the no-penis, would not be limited by any boundary and the frame of reference would have to be provided by something that could fulfil the functions of two axes and a system of co-ordinates. The system of co-ordinates, by making possible a transformation from the visual imagery of geo-metry to the manipulations of algebraic symbols confers greater freedom of investigation and in this respect differs from the frame of reference provided by a state of being inside or outside the state represented by a circle. That state is centred on a no-breast (or point) and is therefore analogous to the geometrical circle, "centred on" its centre (or point).

Column 1 categories are limiting since the definitory hypothesis is to mark a constant conjunction and the exclusion of all previously recorded constant conjunctions (the "negative" quality of definition). The column 3 categories bind a constant conjunction, but the meaning of the constant conjunction does not have to be sought within the domain of the conjoined elements: it must be assumed that the recording aspect of notation is related to the need to find other constant conjunctions which, taken with conjunctions already bound and recorded, yield meanings (that is, relatedness and coherence) hitherto unrecorded. The re-cording aspect of 3 is related to the function of attention that inheres in all column 4 elements.

Freud speaks[1] of the capacity for thinking as affording relief from frustration, in that thought can fill the gap

[1] Freud, S.: *Two Principles of Mental Functioning.* Standard Edition, Vol. XII.

between the time when an impulse is born and its satisfaction. He is referring to action taken by the organism, under the influence of pain, to change its environment. I propose to class the transformation that takes place when thought is expressed in speech as action. Before this transformation thought is restricted to the domain of β-elements, α-elements, and dreams before they are verbalized. But as thought can be used to inhibit action, so definition can be used to inhibit thought. If persecutory feelings are strong the constant conjunction of elements can lead to a naming of the conjunction with intent to contain it, rather than to mark it for investigation. Such motivation, represented by D, approximates to the production of β-elements; but in its less severe forms shows as speech in which nothing can be taken for granted; the term "cat" has no undertones and overtones, whether it is heard or uttered. In talking to a person in whom such a state is active it appears to be impossible to avoid misunderstanding unless words are used with their exact signification. The negative aspect of the definitory hypothesis is strengthened so that the exclusive function of the hypothesis is not a barrier against irrelevance but a denial of the domain to which the hypothesis belongs. For example, the term "cat" would not bind a constant conjunction that excludes "dogginess", but binds a constant conjunction so restrictively that it excludes all animal characteristics. Carried to extremes, the term "cat" is merely a sign analogous to the "point" as the "place where the breast used to be"[1] and should mean the "no-cat". Further denudation leads ultimately to the point which is merely a position without any trace of what used to occupy that position.

There would seem to be no reason why the point or the line should not be regarded as "an abstraction" or an "unknown" in the mathematical sense. It will, or will not, be so regarded according to the use to which it is put (the horizontal axis of the grid). Where I think it is useful to

---

[1] Although I shall continue to speak of the place where something "used to be" I mean it to be understood that the tense is a matter of indifference because, as I said earlier (Chapter 5) the point is also a "now" which has no past or future.

differ from the philosophical or mathematical view is in regarding "abstraction" or "unknown" as designations of stages on the genetic axis.

The point (·) or the line (———) and all substantival terms may, in the view put forward in *Learning from Experience, Elements of Psycho-Analysis*, and this book, be regarded as unknowns having two values: one, a sign for a constant conjunction and the other, a sign for the position, unoccupied, of the object.

Now the object, the constant conjunction, or the position it does *not* occupy, lend themselves to different treatment in that they differ from each other. If the difference can be recognized it becomes possible to elaborate procedures which will turn to good account the properties of the two objects. For convenience I shall distinguish the object from the "position it does not occupy" by signifying the latter by minus signs.

The rules for the manipulation of · and ——— lead to formulations, first through geometrical configurations and then through algebraic transformations of those configurations, that are analogous to pre-conceptions (row D) but belong to row H. These formulations may then be used in accordance with the categories I have set out on the vertical axis; such elaborations depend upon the genetic history of · and ———. This is a dimension of · and ———. They must represent where the · and the ——— used to be or where they will be at some future date. This is denied if time is reduced to a "now" alone with a "future" (that is, where a future used to be, a not-present) and a "past" (that is, where a past used to be and is now a not-present) that are both representations of the wreckage left by splitting attacks on the present. We must next consider the relationship of the no-thing to ideas of space and the no-present to ideas of time.

The — · and — ——— retain meaning, as does the no-thing (because at least there is a trace of whatever it is that does not occupy the position) so long as time itself is not reduced to the moment without a past or a future. But if · represents only a position without duration, it and the corresponding line have become meaningless. In the situation represented by the meaningless · and meaningless ———— the patient can attempt to manipulate the analyst to give interpretations so that the session is used to deny complete meaninglessness and thus to provide reassurance against the dread that all meaning, all source of meaning, has been annihilated. This dread is associated with belief in the breast as the source of meaning as, physically, it is felt to be the source of milk.[1]

The point or line of the geometer may seem indistinguishable from the — · or — ————. In that case the failure to use or develop these objects or — would have to be sought in the relationship of the personality to the · or ———— part of itself. — · and + · are two values of · and the same is true of + and — ————. The transformation is from · or ———— to + or — · and + or — ————. If we use the grid we may replace — · and — ———— by ←̇ ↑ and ←̲ ↑. Such signs represent objects which are devoid of characteristics, lack duration, or position, and, therefore, existence. But the sign ← ↑ indicates that the object is not static. ← ↑ represents a force[2] that continues after · has been annihilated and it destroys existence, time and space.

The state represented by ←̇ ↑ is different from that represented by · or ————. If these signs merely represent the place where the object was or could be there is nothing inherently difficult in supposing that they could be used for thinking about objects *in their absence*. I can make the mark · where I like and I can make another so — — and these marks may then be manipulated into a design according to my predispositions. They may be combined to form a geometrical configuration, or letters of a script, or a drawing. In the latter instance, the recognizable artistic product and the subject it is supposed to portray have features in common that may be called invariants. There may be other invariants common to the artistic production and the no-thing, the thing represented by a · where the thing is not, and

[1] See Chapter 6.
[2] I do not wish to commit myself to the theory that there is a realization approximating to this force.

these invariants are the points and lines actually represented by marks on paper or "seen" (the mental counterpart) with the inward eye.[1] Some suspicion of the existence of this component probably lies in the search to find golden sections and other geometrical figures in, or to impose them on, artistic productions.

The need for rules by which · and ——— are to be regulated if they are to communicate, say, an impression of a landscape, is recognized. The same is true of every form of expression: it is accepted that there must be rules that are to be obeyed in verbal communication, or music, or painting, if the transformation of O is to combine the invariants in such a way that communication with others is effectual. These rules must be such that the no-thing is adequately communicated by a proper combination of the invariants. A work of art should satisfy by a proper disposition of the invariants to O, the no-thing (· or ———) and $T \beta$.

The problem posed by ← ↑ can be stated by analogy with *existing* objects. ← ↑ is violent, greedy and envious, ruthless, murderous and predatory, without respect for the truth, persons or things. It is, as it were, what Pirandello might have called a Character in Search of an Author.[2] In so far as it has found a "character" it appears to be a completely immoral conscience. This force is dominated by an envious determination to possess everything that objects that exist possess including existence itself.

The premiss that the object does not exist would rule out the *existence* of the characteristics I have adumbrated except in the mind of the patient who appears to entertain the phantasy of such a self-contradictory object. But the patient may identify himself with such an object and the contradiction then lies in his existing sufficiently to feel that he does not exist. The rule that a thing cannot both be and not be is inadequate.

The problem is simplified by a rule that "a thing can never

---

[1] See Milton: *Paradise Lost*, Bk. III, "and the mind through all her powers irradiate, there plant eyes. . . ." (lines 51–55).

[2] Pirandello: *Six Characters in Search of an Author.*

be unless it both is and is not". Stating the rule in other forms: "a thing cannot exist in the mind alone: nor can a thing exist unless at the same time there is a corresponding no-thing." The rules that apply to the thing do not apply to the no-thing. Contradiction is not an invariant under psycho-analysis though it may exist in the domain of psycho-analytic objects (which *must* both be and not be).

If there is a "no-thing" the "thing" must exist. By analogy, if Falstaff is a no-thing Falstaff also exists: if it can be said that Falstaff, Shakespeare's character who had no real existence, has more "reality" than people who existed in fact, it is because an actual Falstaff exists: the invariant under psycho-analysis is the ratio of no-thing to thing. But $+ \cdot$ and $- \cdot$ can coincide; in this case the patient who displays a state of mind approximating to this representation regards the analyst who is actually present as also the *place* where the analyst is not. Conversely, the analyst who is actually absent is regarded as a space which is occupied by the absent analyst.[1]

The above description is an approximation. Its relationship with the description that follows is analogical. Using the geometrical visual image I can represent the frame of mind to which I wish to draw attention by the point-pair that is actual and coincident (contrasted with the point-pair that is actual and separate and the point-pair that is conjugate complex). The line on which the coincident pair is situated is tangential to the circle which represents a situation in which "inside" and "outside" exist. The visual image, of the tangent to a circle, can represent a contact with a personality that has an inside and an outside in a manner that makes the $+ \cdot$ and the $- \cdot$ coincident; there is no distinction between the thing and the no-thing though both exist. The personality has contact only at one point: since the point-pair are coincident the contact represents the tenuous relationship seen in patients with disturbances of thought.

The line and circle cut at coincident points can also be

[1] See Hallucinosis, Chapter 5, where I discuss transformations in hallucinosis.

used to represent the relationship between ♀ and ♂ described by me in *Learning from Experience*. If ♂ is replaced by the visual image of the line (———) and ♀ by the visual image of the point (·) the relationship between the two objects, linear and circular (inside and outside), can be expressed by the relative positions of the two points without direct appeal to line or circle. The two points, thing and no-thing, are determined by the fact that they lie on the point of inter-section of line and circle.

From what I have said of ← ↑ the ultimate non-existent "object", the "space" and "time" annihilated object and its all-consuming greed for, and envy of, anything that exists, because it exists, is associated with fear of being the victim of this "space" either as an object that would be devoured by it, or as the servant compelled to provide the ← ↑ (space) with the means with which to satisfy its demand for all that exists. The individual feels himself to be occupying property that belongs to "space". "Space" and the psyche are not felt to be capable of co-existence. Such fears can be seen in analysis of psychotic and claustrophobic patients. The Mad Hatter's tea party in *Alice in Wonderland* is a representation to which this timeless and spaceless "space" approximates.

The analogies which I have sought for the breast and no-breast may be employed again with regard to the space and no-space. Space may be regarded as pure, violent emotion, dominated by greed: no-space as the place where space was. Or, to find another analogy, + space is high pressure, − space or no-space, is low pressure: low pressure devours high pressure, high pressure occupies low pressure.

The relationship of Euclidean geometry to what is ordin-arily called space has often been remarked upon and it has been supposed that in ordinary space, so-called, could be found the realizations that approximate to the theoretical constructions of Euclidean geometry and from thence, at a further remove, the transformation leading to algebraic geometry. In my description I have remarked on certain states in which thought itself has been attacked as being indistinguishable from a no-thing. From this I have pro-ceeded to ←̄, ←̄ ↑, and finally to what I have represented by ← ↑ or emotion + no-emotion, high pressure and low pressure. Geometrical constructions have shown their value in representing the realizations found in geographical space. By proceeding ↞ ↑ I have sought to show that geometrical constructions related to, and strove originally to represent, biological realities such as emotions. The progression represented by ↞ ↑ leads to the possibility that mathematical space may represent emotion, anxiety of psychotic intensity, or repose also of psychotic intensity—a repose more psychiatrically described as stupor. In every case the emotion is to be part of the progression, breast → emotion (or place where breast was) → place where emotion was. I hope that in time the base will be laid for a mathematical approach to biology, founded on the biological origins of mathematics, and not on an attempt to fasten on biology a mathematical structure[1] which owes its existence to the mathematician's ability to find realizations, that approximate to his constructs, amongst the characteristics of the inanimate.

I propose to devote a little time to the relationship of the elements of mathematics to the biological realizations to which they approximate.

[1] See remarks on the golden section, p. 102.

CHAPTER EIGHT

THE domain of thought may be conceived of as a space occupied by no-things; the space occupied by a particular no-thing is marked by a sign such as the words "chair", or "cat" or "point" or "dog". The attempt to free this domain from associations of space perception is supported by use of concepts such as "thought" or "thinking" or "in the mind", but a thought continues to have the penumbra of associations proper to "the place where . . ." the no-thing is. This is also true of feelings and emotions however expressed.

The "objects" with which psycho-analysis deals include the *relationship* of the no-thing and the thing. The personality that is capable of tolerating a no-thing can make use of the no-thing, and so is able to make use of what we can now call thoughts. Since he can do so he can seek to fill the "space" occupied by the thought; this makes it possible for the "thought" of space, line, point to be matched with a realization that is felt to approximate to it. In this respect $\rightarrow$ contrasts with $\leftarrow$ and new uses can be found for $\rightarrow$ that cannot be found for $\leftarrow$. The search for, and discovery of, elements perceived in space is part of the procedure by which elements of category 1 begin to acquire meaning; the negative quality of the definitory hypothesis is discarded or replaced by new elements that saturate the (ξ) elements of $\psi(\xi)$.[1] It is convenient to postulate the existence of a mind represented entirely by points, positions of objects, places where something used to be, or would be at some future date. Objects perceived in space contribute to the transformation of these elements (analogous to ξ) into specific no-things.[2]

On the interplay between the no-thing and the realization that is felt to approximate to it depends the development of thought, and by thought I mean, in this context, that which

[1] *Learning from Experience.*
[2] Similar to the meeting of pre-conception with realization to give rise to conception, but different from it by its closer approximation to the concept of Platonic forms of which the personality is "reminded" by contact with a real object.

enables problems to be solved in the absence of the object. Indeed unless the object is absent there is no problem. The problem is associated with the sense that the realization only approximates to the pre-conception (D1) (or A1, B1, C1). Whether the realization approximates, and if so how closely, depends on a number of factors with which I shall not deal here; with the psychotic personality the approximation has to be extremely close. Consequently (ξ) often remains unsaturated even though the realization does, to ordinary eyes, exist and appears to achieve an adequate degree of approximation to D1. No matter what the reason for the "absence" may be the active no-thing, without a corresponding thing, is associated with dis-satisfaction in the domain of alimentation when hunger exists, but there is no food.

The following may be distinguished from each other: the no-thing and no corresponding realization, the realization, but no corresponding no-thing, the co-incidence of no-thing and thing (the sense-perceived object); this last is inseparable from contact at one point only between a personality (a series of points) and an inside-outside personality ($\therefore$ with a surface) represented by a circle. We shall have to consider shortly the problems of geometrical representation when detached from its genetic developmental association with sense-perceived space and return it to represent the mental domain from which it sprang.[1]

First I consider $\nearrow$ "in search of existence". What this sign represents must be determined by discovery of realizations approximating to it; it is both mental, and susceptible of sense-perception. (Sense-perception must here be contrasted with, and distinguished from, Freud's "consciousness[2] as a sense-organ of psychic quality".)

Having allocated a sign $\nearrow$ which, according to theory, means that there is a constant conjunction that requires to be bound I need to know what the constant conjunction thus represented means. I might as well say that it is because I think there is a constant conjunction that I think there is a meaning. Further, my belief that there is a meaning is itself

---

[1] See Agoraphobia, Chapter 9.
[2] Freud, S.: *Interpretation of Dreams*, Chap. VII. Standard Edition, Vol. V.

one element that is constantly conjoined with other elements in any situation in which a constant conjunction is felt to occur.

It is necessary to suppose that there is awareness of a constant conjunction. Since I have already allocated a meaning to ↙↑ I could attribute awareness of the constant conjunction to it. I shall not however do so. I shall keep it unaltered as a β-element. It may however improve the efficacy of ↙↑ as a form of notation if I, who think that stupor and violent greedy ambition to possess all the qualities of existence have the same configuration, re-write ↙↑ as ± ↙↑.

To return to "awareness". By analogy I would like as a temporary measure to use Cs as a sign for "awareness". It might be useful to attribute this to ± ↙↑, but Cs and − ↙↑ appear to be inconceivable. As I do not wish to be deterred from discussing the point merely because it is inconceivable, I shall assume a Cs that is a β-element (grid category A1), and further that Cs (A1) is or is not inseparable from ± ↙↑ according to the needs of my inquiry. A wish to communicate with others involves consideration of the limitations imposed by that desire.

If I postulate Cs belonging to the category A1 I am assuming it is possible to conceive of a β-element and so to use the *concept* of a β-element although it is impossible to use a β-element itself. Therefore my *concept* of a β-element (category D1, D3, D4) is used as if it were "about" something, that is, as if it had a meaning; that implies that there is, or that I can conceive that there is, a constant conjunction corresponding to my statement "β-element", or, more particularly in this context, Cs (A1).

By analogy with more sophisticated inquiries I can ask what are the properties of Cs (A1); it has none of the qualities ordinarily believed to inhere in the idea of properties. The "properties" of Cs (A1) are analogous to the "properties" of zinc when they are said to be such that zinc combined with sulphuric acid produces zinc sulphate + water. In short, Cs (A1) represents a constant conjunction of relationships.

Cs (A1) is of the nature of a tropism. It involves $\psi(\xi)$ in which (ξ) seeks saturation. This "consciousness" is an awareness of a lack of existence that demands an existence, a thought in search of a meaning, a definitory hypothesis in search of a realization approximating to it, a psyche seeking for a physical habitation to give it existence, ♀ seeking ♂. By analogy with mathematics one may then say that psycho-analysis is concerned with establishing the laws governing relationships of psycho-analytic objects. To express this in a variety of terms: any constant conjunction that *is* apparent, *becomes* apparent; any constant conjunction that is apparent, is; any constant conjunction is a function of the relationships described (broadly) as a conjunction. The quality of any constant conjunction (its properties) is a function of the relationships "within" the conjunction together with the function of its relationship with other constant conjunctions.

If I re-read one of my own notes, knowing it embodies what to me was knowledge when I wrote it, it can seem tautological or to express a meaning so inadequately that if an interval of time separates me from the state of mind in which I wrote it it fails to communicate its message even to myself. Yet its capacity to record is enough to make it possible for me to contrast two different views[1] and thereby see its defects both as a record (column 3) and as a precursor to further investigation (column 4).

A visual impression, as used by Euclid when he relies on deducation from visual representations, would offer some prospect of gain in communicability even if at the loss of logical rigour.[2] I gain something by using ♂↑ instead of a host of analogies, but this must be balanced against the advantages of using analogies instead of ♂↑. Logic, common sense, induction, deduction are terms that often

---

[1] This statement is itself an instance of splitting in time, as a method of achieving correlation.

[2] Logical rigour is an attribute of a particular form of manipulation. Every element, according to its grid category, has its appropriate and most nearly rewarding technique of manipulation. Logicians tend to believe that logical rigour is a *sine qua non*. Hence complete neglect of Newton's theological and mystical pre-occupations as if they had no part in the genesis of, for instance, *Opticks*.

represent mechanisms for bringing an intuition within reach of a realization should one exist. But intuition itself is a function of $\pm \swarrow\uparrow$.

By regarding $\swarrow\uparrow$ as a β-element and replacing Cs by something akin to a tropism I can include in $\swarrow\uparrow$ the counterpart of Cs in an element that is not defined by me as an element of thought.

The importance of such a manoeuvre is that it makes it possible to view consciousness as an element for which, at any of its stages of development, an appropriate grid category can be found.

Hitherto I have used the grid for the categorization of elements which have qualities usually associated with sub-stantives; except for ease of exposition this is not necessary. For example, "consciousness" may be categorized in such a way that the use is emphasized. The grid categories have been left so that the horizontal axis can be extended. Thus: suppose the link to be H and the category D4. Consciousness categorized as link H (D4) would represent a state of hostile (H) scrutiny (D or pre-conception) for the purpose of destructive investigation (column 4). Suppose some method of notation by which the column 4 component is strengthened then consciousness would be categorized to show less sub-stantival and more operator quality.

I have chosen to discuss consciousness deliberately. From the present instance, and from previous discussion of aware-ness associated with tropism, it is evident that a term is needed which may represent the invariant function of consciousness in all grid categories in which it can appear or be placed. I propose to resort to the visual representation afforded by geometrical figures.

First I shall equate the object that I have described as analogous to consciousness with "a point of view". Since I do not wish to identify it with any particular point of view, or indeed with any sense, I shall not consider it to be a point "of view" or "of smell" or "of touch" or "of hearing" but simply as a point. The answer to the question, "point of what?" is then left to be determined by clinical experience; the geometrical point used to indicate the point of central projection in projective geometry will serve as a model. The geometer has succeeded, by transformation of Euclidean geometry and its visual representation into algebraic projective geometry, in freeing his investigations from some of the restrictions imposed by the genetic history of the procedures he uses; so psycho-analysis must be freed from the restrictions imposed by the associations with space and sight by which I look to geometry to simplify exposition. The difficulty is one that has to be resolved whenever past meaning, essential to communication or the rendering of private communication into public communication, has to be made suitable for further investigation. Repeating the present example in grid terms, the problem lies in the change that has to take place when column 3 elements are to be made suitable for functions appropriate to columns 4 and 5, and row H elements must provide models for row C.

Visual representations, sprung from the realm of emotional life, e.g. "Shall I compare thee to a summer's day?" and applied to the realm of realization in space have undergone transformation to make them suitable to their investigatory function, whether for discovery of mathematical objects or suitable husbands or wives and recording them when so discovered: I need to return these procedures to the investigation of what I suspect to be their own origins. The argument is, I think, circular: I am relying on the adequacy of the circle's diameter.

The state I have represented by $- \swarrow\kern-0.6em\nearrow$ is one I can also represent in terms classifiable as C3, thus: $- \swarrow\kern-0.6em\nearrow$ may be personified by a non-existent "person" whose hatred and envy is such that "it" is determined to remove and destroy every scrap of "existence" from any object which might be considered to "have" any existence to remove. Such a non-existent object can be so terrifying that its "existence" is denied, leaving only the "place where it was". This does not solve the problem because the place where it was, the no-thing, is even more terrifying because it has, as it were, been further denied existence instead of being allowed to glut itself with any existence it has been able enviously to find. Denial of the existence of the "place where it was"

only makes matters worse because now the "point", marking
the position of the no-thing, cannot be located.

In accordance with Kleinian theory such an object can
be within the personality of either analyst or analysand.
Furthermore it can be regarded as being projected out
"into" (this point will be reconsidered in a moment) some
other object. Equally it may be the ejecting force, that is,
it may enter into an "existing" object in order to eject the
"existingness".

− ∠↑ may be anywhere. Its position, if known, may
be represented by a point, or, it may be represented by
"space". Space is therefore indistinguishable from feeling
+ or −. ∠↑ may represent stupor ("le silence de ces espaces
infinies m'effraie") or violence.

To consider the state I have just described from another
"point of view"; for reasons already given I do not wish to
commit myself to a "point of" anything. I require an element (category column 3 and 4 and $C \leftrightarrow G$) that is *unsaturated*. It would be useful to postulate unlimited "points
of . . .". I shall use points on the circumference of a circle
to represent unlimited "positions" (formerly points of view)
since it may be useful to be able to indicate direction
"inward" or "outward". Any point or number of points
may then be regarded as vertices of projection. Any point,
including that representing the centre of the circle, may
represent the vertex of projection.

I shall illustrate the clinical use of this scheme by supposing
that the extreme − ∠↑ is the vertex of a central projection.
The clinical realization corresponding to this would be a
patient dominated by bad internal objects with characteristics that I have described approximately above. The
"symptoms" as observed clinically can be represented
"spatially" in this geometric scheme by points that belong
to the projected transformation. Before we can suppose that
this geometric representation is appropriate to the realization
there must be some evidence to justify the supposition that
the transformation is projected to a distance and in a
manner that would make the points on the circumference of
a circle a reasonable representation of symptoms other than

those at the vertex. For example, if the patient showed that he felt that he was identified with the breast and that the transformed elements had been projected on to the inner source of the limiting breast, this might reasonably be regarded by the analyst as an occasion for supposing that this geometric representation was apposite. If my description seems strange to the reader it may help if I remind him that I have chosen an illustration from amongst what I have called projective transformations and that I have distinguished these from rigid transformations in which transference manifestations as usually understood in classical analytic theory appear.

In the example I have given it would be unlikely that — ♂ at a central vertex would project a transformation in a way that made anything so well organized as a circle or a sphere an appropriate representation of the receptor or field for the transformation. It is therefore necessary to consider further the ground of the transformation. What I mean by "receptor" or "field" or "ground" can be most simply grasped by analogy with painting in which the ground for the transformation would be the canvas on to which the transformation was projected. First the analytic situation has been devised to provide conditions in which the patient has a ground on to which he can project, either in the manner of projective transformation, or in the manner of rigid motion. For various reasons, the commonest being disturbances in the analyst, the "analytic situation" can at best only approximate to the desirable.[1] Increasing analytic sophistication in the environment from which patients come will introduce further variations in the nature of analytic situations. Even rigid motion transformations cannot always find an appropriate ground on which transference (in the classical sense) may be detected. I do not propose to discuss this further than to indicate that the ground (or analytic situation) will need more study so as to include

---

[1] Other reasons will probably be discovered when the geometrical approach will demonstrate the "paranoid-schizoid position" of Melanie Klein and the geometer's vector space to be in a relation to each other analogous to the two views of a reversible perspective.

these changes and make it possible to detect transformations into different types of "analytic situation". I propose to discuss the problem of the ground for projective and rigid motion transformations as if it were stable and corresponded to what is regarded in classical analysis as the analytic situation.

So far I have expressed the idea of an analytic situation in column 1 category terms, say D1 or E1. There is rightly an aversion from formulations that seem to indicate a higher degree of scientific sophistication than is possible. Nor is it my intention to do more than explore the possibility of advance.

The idea implicit in the theory of transference is that the analyst is the person on to whom the analysand transfers his images. The theories of Malanie Klein already show that such a medium is not adequate for Tp β in what I have called projective transformations. In particular it does not help the analyst to recognize the elements of projective identification as they appear amidst clinical symptoms and material. The analyst must be able to detect signs of projective identification in a field which, relative to that which obtains in classical theory, is, as it were, multi-dimensional.[1] The analytic situation requires greater width and depth than can be provided by a model from Euclidean space. A patient who, in my view, is displaying projective transformations and requires the use of Kleinian theories for comprehension, also uses a field which is not simply the analyst, or his own personality, or even the relationship between himself and the analyst, but all those and more. He will say ". . . this woman" ". . . this dream" and use other similarly undefined (to the analyst) expressions. As this vagueness is an expression of β-element "thinking" the vagueness is not due to loss of definition but can obtrude because the analyst is in a position analogous to that of a listener to the description of a work of art that has been implemented in materials and on a scale that is not known to him. It is as if he heard the description of a painting, was searching on a canvas for the details represented to him,

---

[1] Vector space, as a mathematical concept, comes as near as possible to representing multi-dimensional objects.

whereas the object had been executed in a material with which he is unfamiliar. Such a patient can talk of a "penis black with rage" or an "eye green with envy" as being visible in a painting. These objects may not be visible to the analyst: he may think the patient is hallucinating them. But such an idea, perhaps sound to the view of a psychiatrist, is not penetrating enough for his work as an analyst. Hallucination may be more profitably seen as a dimension of the analytic situation in which, together with the remaining "dimensions", these objects are sense-able (if we include analytic intuition or consciousness, taking a lead from Freud, as a sense-organ of psychic quality).[1]

To make a step towards definition of this space we consider it to be a $-K$ "space" and contrast it with K "space"—the space in which what is normally regarded as classical analysis takes place and classical transference manifestations become "sense-able". Using once more the analogies (C_3 elements) I have already employed, $-K$ "space" may be described as the place where space used to be. It is filled with no-objects which are violently and enviously greedy of any and every quality, thing, or object, for its "possession" (so to speak) of existence. I do not propose to carry my analogies further than to indicate that $-K$ "space", is the material in which, with which, on which (etc.) the "artist" in projective transformation works. As an analogy with space may easily distort I propose to drop the term and speak of transformation in $-K$.[2]

Can the psycho-analyst find signs that will represent $-K$? They must be such that he is able to work with them and provide the rules for doing so.

It is obviously extremely clumsy to have to repeat terms such as "no-thing", "place where the thing was", ".", "point" and so on. Unless each term can be defined and used with accuracy misunderstandings multiply. Rigid definition would defeat the aim to provide an element unsaturated, but awaiting saturation, in the clinical experience (a D_4 element). It is therefore desirable to use grid

---

[1] Freud, S.: *Interpretation of Dreams.* Chap. VII. Standard Edition, Vol. V.
[2] See below: Platonic forms, Christian Incarnation and Hyperbole.

categories to distinguish between different no-things and to
relate them to the grid categories already proposed. This
can be done by assigning a grid category to a statement and
then assigning a grid category to the category already
determined. Thus a second cycle of categorization is initi-
ated. The process can be continued provided the differences
in cycle are recognized.

CHAPTER NINE

THE visual images and terms employed in the following model are chosen without regard to the sources from which they have been derived.

Two people are present: myself and a patient. I am detached and so is he, though for both of us the experience is important. As he lies on the couch and I sit I imagine that a cloud begins to form rather in the way that clouds can sometimes be seen to form above a hot-point on a summer's day. It seems to be above him. A similar cloud may be visible to him, but he will see it arising from me. These are probability clouds.

Soon other clouds form: some of these are new clouds, some formed from old ones, probability clouds that have changed into possibility clouds. The situation must be conceived of as tense however little appears to be happening. I extend the scope of my model by doing away with the restriction implicit in the term "visual" imagery. "Olfactory image", "auditory image", "tactile image" are absurd terms which however can indicate the direction and scope of freedom I want. To abolish any restriction on absurdity, implicit in the analogies drawn from sense impressions, I shall describe the model as composed of C category elements and assume that tension, like "possibility" and "probability", is apparent[1] even if it is not apparent to any known sense. C category elements are described as visual because it enables me to draw on analogy from the sense of sight to communicate my meaning. The tension which is an essential part of the model is perceptible as are clouds. The clouds have increased; possibility clouds become clouds of doubt. Certainty clouds also appear; clouds of depression, guilt, hope and fear likewise. To every cloud there corresponds its hot point, but the cloud, like its analogue in nature, may have wandered far from it.

I associate pressure with both tension and clouds. The

---

[1] Metaphor? or does tension "appear" visually?

total situation I have tried to describe pictorially I would like to be able to describe odoriferously—as a dog might smell it, and, if he were sufficiently gifted, might delineate it odoriferously. And similarly with all other sensuous media available. Since I wish to find a system of representation that would serve for all these systems, and some of whose existence I am unaware, I seek a system of representation that is unsaturated ($\psi(\xi)$) and will permit of saturation.

Now it will be remembered that in a system in which β-elements dominate, "thoughts" are "things", and I pointed out that β-elements do not lend themselves to use as column 4 elements do because they are already saturated; there can be no pre-conception (row D) that can be *used* as a pre-conception, awaiting the realization that produces a conception, because the β-element is already saturated. We can now see that the defects of the no-thing are precisely these —the "absent" or "non-existent" object occupies the space that should be vacant. The analyst can represent the "no-thing" by a sign that *can* be saturated though the object represented *cannot*.

Using clinical experience to represent the situation just described I may describe it thus: The patient occupies the couch because he is determined that no one else should. His aim is to "saturate" the session so that I cannot work and no one can take *his* place. He employs terms (words, etc.) which are occupied by the meaning that they used to have *but* the meaning has been destroyed (or the term has been denuded of its meaning) so that the terms mark the place where the meaning used to be. This absent meaning (that is nevertheless present), will not permit any meaning to take its place. The verbal communication is therefore one that cannot represent O by virtue of the accepted meaning of the sign employed nor can it represent O by access of meaning through saturation.

Therefore in my search for a system that would represent the chief systems that can be seen to exist in the analytic situation (as I have described it in grid category C1 terms) I must replace the C1 elements, visual images of clouds, analyst, analysand, etc., and replace them by elements approximating to $\psi(\xi)$. It is clear that the C_1 elements must not be denuded because were that to occur they would be replaced by β-elements.

I can do this by using the point $(\cdot)$ to represent the "place where" a some-thing (as contrasted with no-thing) could be, and the line (————) as the locus of a point or the place where a point is going. The analogy is defective because it is saturated by a meaning of movement. I shall try to make it more suitable for thought by considering point $(\cdot)$ and line (————) to represent a relationship thus: the point, $(\cdot)$, "place where", stage, must be conceived of as pertaining to the genetic axis: the line (————) must be conceived of as pertaining to the horizontal axis. A pre-conception, represented by $\cdot$ is a stage of development (a seed, so to speak, is a tree at particular stage of its development: so is a tree). A pre-conception represented by a line (————) is a use (such as D4).

The changes I have had to make throughout this book from analogy to more precise formulation, and from more precise formulation to analogy again, illustrate some of the difficulties with which I am attempting to deal. All these changes are examples of transformation. It may be as well to consider what the value of these transformations can be. With regard to transformation into terms of row C categories one advantage is that the sensuous model has a reality, and that reality an invariant quality, that aids communication. A "circle" expresses a meaning that is at once understood by the person to whom it is addressed. If I mean to use $(\cdot)$ to represent "the place where" or "time when" or "stage of growth" to which an object has attained (so that I am freed of limitations imposed by saturation) it is also true that I assume the existence of invariants under the particular transformation to which I resort. For example: I spoke in my model (row C) of clouds. I replace a cloud by $\cdot$ because I may want to replace this by the idea represented by the term "breast" or "penis", or "flatus" or "sanity" or by a no-thing.

I have spoken of a non-existent malignant, hostile, greedy breast. We may regard these characteristics as, so to speak, inborn, primary, essential: or we may regard them as secondary; or indifferently as primary or secondary, but possessing those qualities by virtue of the accident that that is the point at which we start our story. Bearing in mind that narrative and causation are peculiarities of a mode of communication and may therefore be regarded as T α, the qualities attributed to the breast are quite likely to be a function of the relationship between observer and observed. Consideration of in-born or primary or secondary in this context must not interfere with the possibility that the qualities of any object are a function of its relationships.

Thus, to resort again to C category, one cloud in my model may represent greed, hostility, envy and the hot-point may be the genital (of analyst, of analysand, etc.). This view may depend on a narrative approach and be a function of the fact that the analyst has just observed the object. Or it may be a function of "tension". By this I mean that the total analytic situation may be regarded as a system of energy, such as Freud postulated in his attempt towards a neuro-physiological scientific psychology, in which the sum total remains the same within the system but that the instability of any given part of the system can be seen in rises of "pressure". Using this description as my model (row C) the terms greed, hostile, malignant, may be regarded as T β of an O that is a pressure increase associated with relationships. If so, it is important to find rules for the manipulation of the signs, geometric and other, to be used. The rules for manipulation might be such that the signs, when manipulated in accordance with them, preserve a relationship to each other that represents the pressure changes and other supposed "qualities" of the objects (cloud, etc.).[1] We may also consider to what extent the rules for the manipulation of the signs may themselves find a realization, in the rules governing the relationship of personalities, that approximates to them.

If the qualities represented by point or line are a function

[1] The reader may compare the rules of grammatical construction used in a description of anxiety produced by a domestic crisis with the "laws of nature" governing the production of anxiety by a domestic crisis.

of the relationship between the point and line; if the point is representing a genetic stage and the line the category of use, it is clear that the rules governing the manipulations of point and lines are really governing the relationships between two aspects of the same object—the point. But the use of the term "aspect" in the above sentence and the meaning of the term "use" has now become so obscure that it is better to replace both by the point.

To return to the model on p. 117: the model (represented by verbal signs of C category) of analyst and patient served to communicate by virtue of the rigidity (invariant quality) of the images. This same rigidity meant the model was saturated and therefore unsuitable for use as a pre-conception (column 4 element). The combination of terms such as "hot-point" with other terms such as "cloud" and "probability" denied the model any variety of applicability but restricted its usefulness to one context. Terms such as "probability" and "cloud" are not homogeneous. Can they be replaced by signs that are? Yes: if they are replaced by points.

I am assuming that points were originally the space that had been occupied by a feeling, but had become a "no-feeling" or the space where a feeling used to be. Furthermore I assume that instead of having this "space" occupied by a "no-thing" a "point of view" (vertex of projection) can be found if the "space" may be used as an unsaturated element. Systems of geometry significant in scientific development can be regarded as such unsaturated elements. Euclidean geometry has been found to have many approximations in realizations of space. It is supposed that Euclidean geometry was derived from experience of space. My suggestion is that its *intra-psychic* origin is experience of "the space" where a feeling, emotion, or other mental experience "was".

The rules governing points and lines which have been elaborated by geometers may be reconsidered by reference back to the emotional phenomena that were replaced by "the place (or space) where the mental phenomena were". Such a procedure would establish an abstract deductive system based on a geometric foundation with intuitive psycho-analytic theory as its concrete realization. The statements (i) the resumption by the psyche of an emotional experience that has been detoxicated by a sojourn in the good breast (Melanie Klein) and (ii) the transformation of the emotional experience into a geometrical formulation and the use of this geometrical formulation as the counterpart of a concrete realization for a geometrically based, rigorously formulated, deductive system (possibly algebraic), may now be regarded as the (i) intuitive psycho-analytic and (ii) axiomatic deductive representations of the same process. Both statements are verbal representations of a realization and neither of them is satisfactory; nor is much improvement likely by mastery of the medium of verbal expression. The intuitive statement lends itself to the representation of genetic stages: the axiomatic formulation lends itself to the representation of a use.

This distinction points to a similarity between the weakness of the element suitable for representing a genetic stage to the weakness of the β-element. The element that represents genetic stages appears to have or to require a capacity for saturation, for becoming pregnant. I have phrased my last sentence in terms that illustrate the difficulty that arises when a term that in some contexts gains by its metaphorical quality (a "pregnant statement") loses communicative quality if it is employed in a context where its metaphorical quality ceases to be metaphorical because its context has approximated it to a β-element—it is, relative to its context, saturated. Some psychotic patients show skill in manipulating the analytic situation to bring this about. Therefore the element employed requires to have a high saturation point in its context.

The psychotic patient will show fear of an element with a high saturation point because a high capacity for saturation is felt as indistinguishable from greed in the element. That is, if I speak to him using terms in what I consider to be an ordinary conversational sense, and he thinks, perhaps rightly, that I am wishing to elicit information, he will react as if he thought I was trying to take away, not information but his sanity. His reply will be what sounds to me nonsense but is his method of parting with rubbish, or making splitting attacks on my speech. If the latter, his sentences are felt by him to be split into words but each word then becomes a greedy, unsaturated (that is, meaningless and schizophreno-genetic) element in return. The presenting objects are further attacked and become more malignant and minute till finally they qualify to be represented by my sign — ← ↑ for non-existent existence-greedy objects. Can this example from experience provide a starting point for transforming the model into something more scientific?

Agoraphobia is a psychiatric term for a state of mind found in some patients. In my terms it is a name "binding" a constant conjunction. If a patient presenting such symptoms is investigated psycho-analytically we find an extremely complex personality; this in itself is of no significance but for the fact, relevant to this discussion, that I am soon unable to use the term agoraphobia in a way that is meaning-ful: the conjunction is not of the elements that first appeared to compose it nor are they constant. I need to continue using this term, and with it the term "claustrophobia". I therefore assume that, both for the reader and myself, the term binds a constant conjunction.

In analysis it appears that the patient has terrible feelings when he is in open spaces or if he feels shut in.

I propose to use some of the ideas I have been putting forward in this book, as follows: The patient is coming to me for help and one reason for his distress is that his formu-lation does not afford scope for solution of his problem. With an actual case I would not attach importance to this, but in this discussion I shall suppose he is stating *his* experi-ence inadequately for *my* purpose which is to know what he is talking about and to meditate upon it. (What he is talking about = O.) I therefore transform his statement thus: the patient, experiencing "terrible" feelings with the intensity of emotion of an infant having painful feelings, supposes them to be some bad object, perhaps part of himself, if he thinks he has a self, perhaps not. Mobilizing his adult armoury of speech he says he cannot possibly describe his feelings and then proceeds to do so. Since they are indescribable that itself indicates that the feelings described cannot be the ones that were felt. The patient may continue his description: "lost", "shut in", "panic", etc. I can match his diversity of terms with a diversity of my own: "depersonalized", "internal object", etc. For my purposes I want terms which will always be right in all situations in which the problems have the same configuration. Patients and analysts are constantly using different terms to describe situations that appear to have the same configuration. I want to find invariants, under psychoanalysis, to all of them. This condition is almost filled by the term "place where the thing was" or "space". Almost, but not quite. Its virtue can be seen in the fact that it will do equally well for agoraphobia or claustrophobia, and to that extent avoids two terms for configurations that are only apparently different. What is needed is a solution that will dispose finally of the diversity of terms, at present required to describe the experience called "claustro- or agoraphobia", and the far more serious defect associated with it, namely, the elaboration of as many theories as there are sufferers, matched by almost as many theories as there are therapists, when it is acknowledged that the configurations are probably the same. The solution required will cover more than claustrophobia and agoraphobia which I have chosen as a starting point. I choose "space" to represent, on the one hand, emotions which are felt to be indistinguishable from the "place where something was", and on the other, space akin to the geometric realization from which Euclidean geometry is believed to derive.

Certain peculiarities of the problem I am attempting to state are inherent in the problem. Thus I state, as part of an intuitive psycho-analytic theory, that the patient has an experience, such as an infant might have when the breast is withdrawn, of facing emotions that are unknown, unrecognized as belonging to himself, and confused with an object which he but recently possessed. Further descriptions only add to the multiplicity of which I already complain as the reader will see if he consults any analytic descriptions of infantile behaviour. The relationship of these representations with the realizations approximating to them may be compared with the axiomatic geometric deductive space that I wish to introduce as a step towards formulations that are precise, communicable without distortion, and more nearly adequate to cover all situations that are basically the same. I suggest the following comparisons: (i) "Unknown", in the model afforded by the intuitive psycho-analytical theory, with "unknown", in the mathematical sense in which I wish to use "geometric space". (ii) "Variable", as applied to the sense of instability and insecurity in the model of infantile anxiety, with "variable", as I wish to apply it to geometric space. Thus geometric space may represent and be replaced by constant values for any particular universe of discourse. The relationship of geometric space to the psycho-analytic intuitive theory that I propose as *its* realization; the further relationship of the psycho-analytical intuitive theory to the clinical experience which I consider is *its* realization; together these represent a progression such as that in the transformation of an experience into a poem—"emotion recollected in tranquillity." The geometric transformation may be regarded as a representation, "detoxicated" (that is, with the painful emotion made bearable) of the same realization as that represented (but with the painful emotion expressed), by the intuitive psycho-analytical theory. This implies that any individual capable of making the transformation from O, when O is a psychic reality, to T β is capable of doing for himself something analogous to projective identification into the good breast, he being identified with himself and the breast.

There are further similarities to which I want to draw attention: if it is accepted that geometric space affords a link between unsophisticated emotional problems, their unsophisticated solutions and the possibility of their restatement in sophisticated terms admitting of sophisticated solutions, then it may be that musical and other artistic methods afford a similar link. These must not be regarded as replacements of the geometric approach. The investigation must be directed to the elucidation of point and line as elements imbedded in the material of transformations in the media of all arts and sciences. In the poem it may be found in the long–short of rhythm; in painting it may be found, not as Vitruvius sought to find it, in a golden section or other geometric plan, as the method of construction, but in the matter from which the construct is formed. In music it may be looked for not in musical notation, but music itself. In science it may be seen in the atomic theories of Democritus of Abdera.

The grid provides a scheme whereby visual images of category C may be seen to have counterpart in H category, and vice versa. The categories reserved for mathematical representations only may be open to sophisticated versions of auditory, visual, or other forms of C category representation. Thus certain paintings, or musical compositions, could properly be considered to fall in H categories together with certain algebraic formulations, if their invariants were recognized and their relationships seen to conform to rule.

This discussion is concerned with such representations, whatever the discipline, as having disposed within them the invariants of point and line; intuitive psycho-analytical theory is its corresponding realization.

CHAPTER TEN

THIS chapter is a review and summary. I begin with a model of transformation: suppose a number of marbles of different colours and sizes, $\frac{1}{2}''$, $\frac{3}{4}''$ and $1''$ in diameter, lying in a tray. The colours and sizes are "dimensions". Make a rule that in another tray must be placed as many marbles of $1''$ diameter as there are green marbles in the first tray. When the operation has been completed the marbles in the second tray will represent a transformation of the "space" represented by the marbles of different size and colour in the first tray. The collection on the first tray represents the "space" I have denoted O. The rule regulating the disposition of marbles on the second tray represents the mental activity I have denoted by T α (or T aα if it governs the behaviour of the analyst). The marbles on the second tray represent the transformation I have denoted T β (or T aβ if effected by the analyst).

I may now use the marbles on the second tray as the O for further transformation. I can denote this by writing O (2nd cycle) = T aβ (1st cycle). I make a rule that on another tray are to be placed as many marbles of $1''$ diameter as there are blue marbles on the second tray. This rule may accordingly be denoted T aα (2nd cycle) and when the operation is complete the marbles on the third tray represent a state I denote by the sign T aβ (2nd cycle). This can now be made the starting point of a further operation which is similar to the two preceding but is now the third cycle of transformation.

The foregoing model I shall replace by one that comes nearer to representing an analytic experience, thus: suppose the patient makes a complex statement, in the sense I have given the term, which may have consisted of anything from a solitary ejaculation to a session of free associations. I shall suppose that the statement is so complex that it would only be adequately represented by being categorized in every grid category. The categories, like the sizes and colours of the marbles, may be regarded as "dimensions" of the statement. In practice, the patient's behaviour can fairly easily be seen to fall into two or three categories and analysts are familiar with the problem of trying to decide what aspect of the material should be regarded as immediately significant and interpreted accordingly. Use of the grid makes it possible to scan the analytic material methodically. At first it is wise to use it retrospectively so that nothing should interfere with the analyst's absorption of the evidence. Practice in review of analytic work by this method leads quite soon to facility in unconscious and immediate assessment of evidence as it unfolds in the session. The hypothetical statement of my model has facets qualifying it for every grid category. I have previously said[1] that it is important to play psycho-analytic games as a part of the daily review of analytic work, and one valuable game consists in supposing what the interpretations would have been and what course the analyst might have taken if, instead of the actual conjectures and interpretations, the material had been categorized quite differently. Stating this in terms of transformation theory the statement is regarded as a field of diverse dimensions with which we are required to deal. We may choose column 2 elements as most significant and ignore all other categories that are present. The interpretation which we base on the dimension thus isolated will be denoted $T\,a\beta$. O, corresponding to the first tray of marbles in model 1, will be the total statement. The decision to choose column 2 elements, as more significant than all others, corresponds to the rule determining how the marbles were to be disposed on the second tray; it is accordingly denoted by $T\,a\alpha$. The interpretation is the transformed statement and corresponds to the marbles on tray 2.

At first this rule appears arbitrary compared to the rule in model 1 because it can be argued that $T\,a\alpha$, in model 2, is merely a decision to ignore one set of facts in favour of another. Yet the rule in model 1 is no less arbitrary although an appearance of legality is conferred by an appeal to the

[1] In *Elements of Psycho-Analysis*.

contents of tray 1 as decisive in determining the contents of tray 2.

The difference in the two models consists in the fact that in model 2 the rule makes the point of arbitrary change explicit. The fact that there are so many green marbles in tray 1 is used to decide the number of marbles of 1″ diameter in the second. No more explanation is given for this than for ignoring all dimensions save column 2 in the second model.

In model 2 the interpretation (T aβ) should be associated with a K link; the analyst is concerned to understand the associations and to communicate that understanding to the patient. The patient in accordance with our postulate is the source of an L, H or −K link. But, since he comes voluntarily it must be assumed that his associations are also intended to be part of a K link.

The conclusion must be that we must make assumptions about assumptions about . . . *ad infinitum.* No conclusion is possible about the arbitrary nature of the rule. The rule may be seen however to be a special case of the pre-conception. It is a formulation representing a pre-conception and it is used in accordance with column 4. The provisional category for the rule is D4. If we suppose that the rule is intended to *do* something we attribute to it the quality of an act and the category would be more correctly D6.

T aα is a private process limited to the analyst's mind: the categorization of T aα impinges on the domain of counter-transference and the analyst's own analysis. The matter is relevant to discussion of the nature of the relationship of interpretations to the matter interpreted. The assumption underlying loyalty to the K link is that the personality of analyst and analysand can survive the loss of its protective coat of lies, subterfuge, evasion and hallucination and may even be fortified and enriched by the loss. It is an assumption strongly disputed by the psychotic and *a fortiori* by the group, which relies on psychotic mechanisms for its coherence and sense of well-being. Discussion of this assumption will lie on the periphery of the theme of transformations which I take next.

Treating my hypothetical statement, with dimensions represented by all grid categories, as the subject for the psycho-analytical game, I wish to consider the implications of ignoring all aspects (dimensions) of the statement save those that fall in category A6. I shall assume that it is not obligatory to do this and that many correct interpretations could be seen to be available from an ordinary scansion of the other grid dimensions, the dimensions I propose to ignore. I wish it to be supposed that if a layman could hear the patient he would not feel completely at a loss to understand though he might easily be aware that there was something he did *not* understand and be puzzled to know why. I also wish it to be supposed that the only reason for questioning the soundness of an analysis based on classical analytic theories would be the bizarre response to interpretations which would appear to be quite correct. By bizarre I mean that the patient's response does not saturate the analyst's pre-conceptions but appears itself to require saturation. In conditions such as these, postulated to facilitate psychological preparation for the theories that follow, the psycho-analytical game may develop the analyst's intuition (as a musician's exercises facilitate his capacity to perform an actual musical creation though not themselves being more than scales and other manual exercises) in preparation for the work required of it in analysis.

My aim is to illustrate a particular form of transformation and to approach it by consideration of the elements of a statement and its dimensions, notably the dimension bound by me by the term β-element, as manipulated in a mental domain where thoughts are not distinguished from things and the mind is felt to operate as if it were a muscle.

As I am assuming the grid category is A6 I shall not consider the significance of what is said to reside predominantly in the meanings of the words and sentences as it would do if I regarded the communication made by the patient as part of a rigid motion transformation. I expect it to be significant that the patient in the course of speaking expels air from his lungs. His failure to distinguish thoughts from things contributes to a sense that the actual meaning of the words, as that would be understood in a rigid motion transformation, is expelled as air from his lungs is expelled. Conformably with this the patient seems to feel that his mind is an expelling organ like a lung in act of expiration. Were I regarding his communication as part of a rigid motion transformation I should hear him say something like this: "Whatever has happened to my key? It can't be six unless the milkman came early. The rounds are impeccable as a rule though my friend said it was quite different her way. You think you are wonderful but you are just a thief."

As I am supposing that his communication is part of a projective transformation composed of A6 elements, I consider that some "thing" is being evacuated. The "thing" may be the scene in the consulting room. In that case the patient is using his eyes, and the mental counterpart of his capacity for vision, as evacuatory musculature. What to me appears to him to be the product of a visual evacuation.

The "thing" may be something adumbrated by his words —if I may assume I am correct in allowing myself to gain an impression based on what *I* think his words should mean if he were talking conversational English. Such an impression is based on long experience of the patient's communications and on acceptance of them as row A formulations of a highly idiosyncratic type. What my assumptions amount to is that the communication is a mixture in which a meaning, grasped by ordinary modes of understanding, has been treated by the patient as if it were a thing, and evacuated phonetically and mentally as if by an apparatus whose characteristics are those usually associated with muscles.

I cannot attempt a detailed description of how or why I arrive at the qualities which I am about to attribute to the evacuated object. The F category meanings can be expressed approximately as follows: "the key, that which gives potency and is itself capacity or potency, has gone. The coming of the milkman could tell me the time—six o'clock. The time, six o'clock, could tell me the milkman was coming. The milkman's ejaculation (coming) could tell me the time and feed me. But none of these things happens. The key has been lost; they have been denuded of their meaning. I know this is because I am self-supporting because I can hallucinate a meal, time, an ejaculation and whatever else I need. Then, from these evacuated objects (hallucinations in the analyst's opinion) I can gain all the mental and physical sustenance I require. But I am unable to get such sustenance. Obviously, therefore, what you, the analyst, call psycho-analysis is simply your method of stealing the sustenance from my hallucinations, leaving me without a key, while you are able to feel how superior your psycho-analysis is and how clever you are. But psycho-analysis is not superior to my hallucinations. You only make it appear so by stealing the goodness from hallucinations so they seem bad mental faeces and psycho-analysis is made good."

My account of these events cannot be made plausible to anyone who has not had the analyst's experience. I shall not attempt to make the description convincing but shall pass on to consider implications of this and similar ineffable experiences.

Although I have said I proposed to play my psycho-analytical game on the assumption that all elements were A6 my introduction of the mixed association in which F row elements were being treated as if they belonged to A row shows, as anyone might reasonably expect, that nothing in the practice of psycho-analysis ever fits into neat and rigid categorizations. Nevertheless the grid categories do make it possible to draw attention to find shades of difference in meaning in a way which would be difficult or impossible without them—as in this instance where relatively sophisticated elements are being treated in a manner much more suited to the primitive and immature.

As a result of treating the elements of the statement as A6 certain factors peripheral to A6 elements can be seen to be activated and can be detected in analysis.

(i) Hallucination is seen as a method of achieving independence which the patient considers to be superior to psycho-analysis.

(ii) Its failure, in so far as it is seen as a failure, is attributed to the rivalry, envy and thieving propensities of the analyst.

(iii) Rivalry, envy, greed, thieving, together with his

sense of being blameless, deserve consideration as invariants under hallucinosis.

(iv) The concept of hallucinosis needs to be widened to fit a number of configurations which are at present not recognized as being the same.

(v) Transformation, in rigid motion or projection, must be seen to have hallucinosis as one of its media.

(vi) The rules of transformation in hallucinosis must be established through clinical observation. I have no doubt that they exist and can be delineated by observation of the operation envy, greed, rivalry, "moral" and scientific superiority in hallucinosis. I offer the following suggestions provisionally as an example of such "rules".

A. If an object is "top" it dictates "action"; it is superior in all respects to all other objects and is self-sufficient and independent of them.

B. Objects that can occupy such a position include (*a*) Father, (*b*) Mother, (*c*) Analyst, (*d*) Aim, object or ambition, (*e*) Interpretation, (*f*) Ideas, whether moral or scientific.

C. The only relationship between two objects is that of superior to inferior.

D. To receive is better than to give.

Similarly it is possible to formulate a mathematics of hallucinosis. I offer the following suggestions formulated to give first a description of the emotional background and second the arithmetical statement. In rigid motion transformation:

a^1 The infant feels it is being satisfied by the breast: the breast disappears and the satisfaction with it.

a^2 1 breast + 0 breast = 0 breast

a^3 1 + 0 = 0

Suppose now that the personality cannot tolerate frustration. This is associated with "that state of mind in which ideas may be supposed to assume the force of sensations through the confusion of thought with the objects of thought, and the excess of passion animating the creations of imagination"[1]

---

[1] Shelley, P. B.: Hellas. His sixth note on the poem.

(I use Shelley's formulation of his poetic intuition to provide the background realization for the statement "hallucinosis"). Memory of the satisfaction is used to deny the absence of satisfaction. Denial of time is used to deny that the breast is the place where the breast used to be and to maintain that it is where the breast now is. The mathematical transformation in hallucinosis may be stated thus (b^2 taking the place of a^2, etc.):

b^2 1 breast + 0 breast = 1 breast
b^3 1 + 0 = 1.

There may be good reasons for supposing that $1 + 0 = 1$, for example that there is a realization that may approximate to it and the formulation $1 + 0 = 1$ may help to establish a K link with such a realization. But b^3 is intended to demonstrate the relationship between 0 and 1 in a domain where it is possible to remove the "noughtness" from 0 and so produce 1. Therefore in the domain of hallucinosis $0 - 0 = 1$. It is natural to wonder what would be the result of adding nought to nought. It is $0 + 0 = 0^0$. That is to say that if noughtness is added to noughtness the noughtness is multiplied by itself. The emotional state that might provide a background realization approximating to this is the state of complete freedom from the restriction imposed by contact with realizations of any kind. The ability of 0 to increase thus by parthogenesis corresponds to the characteristics of greed which is also able to grow and flourish exceedingly by supplying itself with unrestricted supplies of nothing.

These mathematical manipulations serve a purpose in the domain of hallucinosis analogous to that served by mathematics in D4 and 5 investigations where frustration exists. In hallucinosis nought denuded of its noughtness is hostile envious and greedy and does not even exist as it is denuded of its existence.

The realizations which form the background of hallucinosis differ from those that form the background in the domain of accepted frustration. (To save time I shall denote the latter by f and the former by h.) In f, 1 breast +

0 breast + 1 breast + 0 breast + 1 breast + 0 breast + 1 breast + 0 breast = −4 breasts. Or: 1 + 0 + 1 + 0 + 1 + 0 + 1 + 0 = −4. In *h*, 1 breast + 0 breast = "one breast denuded of existence" and "a place where the breast was, also denuded of existence" = a raging inferno of greedy non-existence.

If we compare 1 in *f* mathematics with 1 in *h* mathematics, it can be seen in *f* to be a dimension of a statement even though the statement of which it is a dimension is not known and may be a realization whose existence is revealed only by the existence of this one dimension. In *h*, 1 is a column 2 element and is intended and understood to mean that an object is devoid of dimensions because it has dimensions that are to be rendered incapable of transformation. To be incapable of transformation the statement must be denuded of dimensions, rules must be made incapable of regulation (in other words denuded of any dimensions that qualify rules to be regarded as rules) and vertices must be destroyed. For analytic practice this means that any efforts that the analyst makes towards establishing dimensions, rules or vertices, or establishing that such dimensions, rules and vertices exist, will be under attack. Amongst such procedures will be projective identification placed in a vertex so that it will be inoperable; thus a part of the patient's personality will occupy "the place of" the analyst to deny that vertex to the analyst. This leads me to reconsider some aspects of that particular form of transformation known to analysts as the interpretation.

For a greater part of its history it has been assumed that a psycho-analytic interpretation had as its function the rendering conscious of that which is unconscious. The relatively simple division of elements into conscious and unconscious has proved extremely fruitful, but it no longer provides a satisfactory criterion of an interpretation to regard it as either making or failing to make that which is unconscious conscious. With the grid it is possible to categorize a statement, its interpretation, and the statement that is a resultant of the two. Can the relationship between the categories to which statements are assigned provide a more illuminating approach than the relationship conscious:unconscious?

In the three models of transformation that I have sketched out in this chapter (A1, B1 and B2) O, T aα and T pα, T aβ and T pβ, can be distinguished. The medium in the first is provided by marbles and trays, in the second by the relationship between analyst and analysand (as subject to manipulation by the patient to make it fit in the framework of hallucinosis) and in the third by the relationship between analyst and analysand as subject to representation so that the representation could be manipulated as part of a K link.

The difference between B1 and B2 makes it likely that the statements of the analysand will differ in category from those of the analyst, for the medium of the analysand's transformation lies in the sphere of action, that of the analyst in the sphere of thought and its verbal representations.

The patient whose transformations are effected in the medium of hallucinosis might almost have as his motto "actions speak louder than words" with its hint of rivalry as an essential feature of the relationship. The analyst appears to be offered the choice of abandoning his technique, which is an admission of surrender to the superior wisdom and technique of the analysand, or, keeping to analysis and thereby showing by *his* actions that *he* considers *his* technique superior; either course would fit in with an acting out of rivalry.

The statement "acting out of rivalry" in my last sentence will serve as an example of the distorting effect produced by the approach to a configuration through one of its parts. Rivalry is an important element but its significance depends on the particular constant conjunction or configuration of which it is a part. "Rivalry" signifies a constant conjunction but the constant conjunction it signifies is not the relevant one in this context. It is common to find some feature, such as the cruelty of the super-ego, and to suppose that one has discovered the key to a baffling situation only to find that the same feature occurs in other situations which bear no marked resemblance to the situation to which one hoped the key had been discovered. In my experience this difficulty arises because the *key* has been detected in the elements of a second, third or subsequent cycle of psycho-analytic (that is, analyst's) transformations when it should be sought in the nature of the transformations effected by the analysand. What matters in the present context is not rivalry so much as rivalry under transformations in hallucinosis. I shall therefore devote further attention to expanding what I mean by this term without troubling over-much to make the description rigorous. The general picture the patient presents is that of a person anxious to demonstrate his independence of anything other than his own creations. These creations are the results of his supposed ability to use his senses as organs of evacuation which are able to surround him with a universe that has been generated by himself: the function of the senses and their mental counterpart is to create the patient's perfect world. Evidence of imperfection is *ipso facto* evidence for the intervention of hostile envious forces. Thanks to the patient's capacity for satisfying all his needs from his own creations he is entirely independent of anyone or anything other than his products and therefore is beyond rivalry, envy, greed, meanness, love or hate; but the evidence of his senses belies his pre-determinations; he is *not* satisfied.

We may now reconsider the term "hallucination". It must be distinguished from an illusion or delusion because both these terms are required to represent other phenomena, namely those that are associated with pre-conceptions that turn to conceptions because they mate with realizations that do not approximate to the pre-conceptions closely enough to saturate the pre-conception, but closely enough to give rise to a conception or mis-conception. The pre-conception requires saturation by a realization that is *not* an evacuation of the senses but has an existence independent of the personality. The hallucination arises from a pre-determination and requires satisfaction from (*a*) an evacuation from the personality and (*b*) from conviction that the element *is* its own evacuation. Confusion occurs if due weight is not given to the fact that the total conjunction bound by the term hallucination is associated with two different points of view, or, as I prefer to call it, with two different vertices, one represented by the patient, the other by the analyst.

To understand the nature of the difference between the two vertices it will be necessary to review phenomena that I class as D1, D2, D3. The intuitive psycho-analytic background is that which I have "bound" by terms such as pre-conception, definition, notation, attention. My object in using grid categories is to escape from the trammels imposed by the penumbra of associations that these terms possess; in the course of this digression I shall say something more of the term pre-determination which I introduced to represent a phenomenon of hallucinosis. I shall borrow freely any material that is likely to simplify my task, starting with Plato's theories of Forms. As I understand the term, various phenomena, such as the appearance of a beautiful object, are significant not because they are beautiful or good but because they serve to "remind" the beholder of the beauty or the good which was once, but no longer is, known. This object, of which the phenomenon serves as a reminder, is a Form. I claim Plato as a supporter for the pre-conception, the Kleinian internal object, the inborn anticipation. Melanie Klein objected in conversation with me to the idea that the infant had an inborn pre-conception of the breast, but though it may be difficult to produce evidence for the existence of a realization that approximates to this theory, the theory itself seems to me to be useful as a contribution to a vertex I want to establish. Phenomena, the term being used as Kant might use it, are transformed into representations, $T \beta$. $T \beta$ may then be regarded as a representation of the individual's experience O, but the significance of O derives from and inheres in the Platonic Form.

The object represented by the term Platonic Form may also be represented in mystical terms such as "One is one and all alone and ever more shall be so", and those of canto xxxiii of the Paradiso. (Barbara Reynolds's translation.)

> "Eternal Light, that in Thyself alone
>   Dwelling, alone dost know Thyself, and smile
> On Thy self-love, so knowing and so known!"

The emphasis is altered by Christian Platonism so that the balance between the elements of the configuration is altered; this may be seen most clearly expressed in the doctrine of the Incarnation. The particular representation which is significant for this discussion has been formulated by Meister Eckhart and the Blessed John Ruysbroeck who distinguish the Godhead from God; thus in Tractate XI "God in the Godhead is spiritual substance, so elemental that we can say nothing about it."

It is evident that in this view God is regarded as a Person independent of the human mind. The phenomenon of Good or Beauty would not then be that which "reminds" the personality of a Form (pre-conception) but is an incarnation of a part of an independent Person, wholly outside the personality, to whom the phenomena are "given". The phenomenon does not "remind" the individual of the Form but enables the person to achieve union with an incarnation of the Godhead, or the thing-in-itself (or Person-in-Himself).

For convenience I shall refer to these two configurations as "Forms" and "Incarnation". In both there is a suggestion that there is an ultimate reality with which it is possible to have direct contact although in both it appears that each direct contact is possible only after submission to an exacting discipline of relationships with phenomena, in one configuration, and incarnate Godhead in the other. In neither is there discussion of establishing a direct contact with the reality of absolute evil, though it is possible that some of the "repellant" quality attributed to St John of the Cross may be an unconscious tribute to his identification of absolute real evil with absolute real good.

The object of this digression, as of the previous discussions in this chapter and book, is to arrive at a postulate. The postulate is that already designated by O. To qualify O for inclusion amongst the column 1 categories by defining its definitory qualities I list the following negatives: Its existence as indwelling has no significance whether it is supposed to dwell in an individual person or in God or Devil; it is not good or evil; it cannot be known, loved or hated. It can be represented by terms such as ultimate reality or truth. The most, and the least that the individual person can do is to be it. Being identified with it is a measure of distance from it. The beauty of a rose is a phenomenon betraying the ugliness of O just as ugliness betrays or reveals the existence of O. L, H, K are links and by virtue of that fact are substitutes for the ultimate relationship with O which is not a relationship or an identification or an atonement or a reunion. The qualities attributed to O, the links with O, are all transformations of O and *being* O. The rose *is* itself whatever it may be *said* to be. The human person *is* himself and by "is" I mean in both instances a positive act of being for which L, H, K are only substitutes and approximations.

Any formulation, including this one, is a representation and all representations are transformations, often of transformations. Any analytic statement can be represented by the sign T aβ (cycle n) or T pβ (cycle n).

O, representing the unknowable ultimate reality can be represented by any formulation of a transformation—such as "unknowable ultimate reality" which I have just formulated. It may therefore seem unnecessary to multiply representations of it; indeed from the psycho-analytic vertex that is true. But I wish to make it clear that my reason for saying O is unknowable is not that I consider human capacity unequal to the task but because K, L, or H are inappropriate to O. They are appropriate to transformations of O but not to O. To recapitulate:

Transformations may be scientific, aesthetic, religious, mystical, psycho-analytical. They may be described as psychotic and neurotic also, but though all these classifications have a value it does not appear to me that the value that they have is psycho-analytically adequate. I have chosen to write, though briefly, of transformation in hallucinosis because the description may serve to explain why I consider existing methods of observation, notation, attention and curiosity are inadequate, why a theory of transformations may aid in making these methods more nearly adequate and why the theory of transformations itself must be freed from existing associations if it is to be fitted for its psycho-analytic tasks. The suggestion of projective transformations differentiated from rigid motion transformations is but one step to indicate the possibilities. The subject cannot be pursued further without considering the relationship between categories of patient's transformations and categories of analyst's transformations. These last I have said must be transformations in K and this leads me to a peculiarity of transformations in K.

It is a commonplace that any attempt at scientific inquiry involves distortion through the exaggeration of certain elements in order to display their significance. This characteristic is present in L and H as much as in K. In order to link its phenomenological counterpart in analytic practice, with the penumbra of associations that I regard as significant, I shall call this characteristic hyperbole. I mean the term to convey an impression of exaggeration, of rivalry and, by retention of its original significance, throwing and outdistancing. The appearance of hyperbole in any form must be regarded as significant of a transformation in which rivalry, envy and evacuation are operating. There is a profound difference between "being" O and rivalry with O. The latter is characterized by envy, hate, love, megalomania and the state known to analysts as acting out, which must be sharply differentiated from acting; which is characteristic of "being" O.

Just as exaggeration is helpful in clarifying a problem so it can be felt to be important to exaggerate in order to gain the attention necessary to have a problem clarified. Now the "clarification" of a primitive emotion depends on its being contained by a container which will detoxicate it.[1] In order to enlist the aid of the container the emotion must be exaggerated. The "container" may be a "good breast", internal or external, which is able to detoxicate the emotion. Or the container may not be able to tolerate the emotion and the contained emotion may not be able to tolerate neglect. The result is hyperbole. That is to say, the emotion that cannot tolerate neglect grows in intensity, is exaggerated to ensure attention and the container reacts by more, and

[1] See Bion, W. R.: *Elements of Psycho-Analysis*, p. 27.

still more, violent evacuation. By using the term "hyperbole" I mean to bind the constant conjunction of increasing
force of emotion with increasing force of evacuation. It is
immaterial to hyperbole what the emotion is; but on the
emotion will depend whether the hyperbolic expression is
idealizing or denigrating.

When the presenting problem in analysis is the hallucinations of the patient a crux has been reached. In addition to
the problem that the patient is attempting to solve by
transformation in hallucinosis is the secondary problem
presented by his method of solution. This secondary problem
appears in analysis as a conflict between the method employed by the analyst and the method employed by the
patient. The conflict can be described as a disagreement on
the respective virtues of a transformation in hallucinosis and
a transformation in psycho-analysis. The disagreement is
coloured by the patient's feeling that the disagreement
between patient and analyst is a disagreement between rivals
and that it concerns rival methods of approach. Unless this
point is made clear no progress can be made. When it has
been made clear the disagreement still continues but it
becomes endo-psychic: the rival methods struggle for
supremacy within the patient. The characteristics of the
conflict are easier to discern when externalized as a conflict
between analyst and patient and this can lead to a collusion
between the two for the patient finds it more tolerable and
the analyst easier. As the conflict involves the nature of the
contributions made by both, I shall use the grid to elucidate
the difference between the two.

As I have said the patient's contributions are A6. The
"rules" according to which he manipulates these elements
are (i) He needs no analyst because he provides the material
for his own cure and knows how to obtain the cure from it.
(ii) The material is evacuated by the mental counterpart
(as the analyst would believe) of his sensory equipment.
(iii) Painful experience is not cure, any more than pleasure,
but both are methods of scoring points in a rivalry relationship. (iv) The relationship between the contestants is
designed to prove the superiority of the patient and

hallucinosis over the analyst and psycho-analysis. (v) "Cure" is identical with "winning".

Following from these "rules" certain anomalies arise: Any benefit achieved as a result of analytic cure is vitiated by its being indistinguishable from "defect" of the analysand. Any victory of the analysand is vitiated by perpetuating the painful status quo. The painful element is due to the obtrusion of the analyst—"the analyst's fault". The analyst's "fault" in the eyes of the analysand is attributable to a two-fold source: (i) All his "interpretations" are A6 elements evacuated by him as a part of his resort to the patient's methods and employment of transformation in hallucinosis; (ii) All his interpretations are psycho-analytic elements designed to prove the superiority of himself and psycho-analysis. In so far as he is guilty of (i) his actions as a psycho-analyst are "acting out"; and of (ii) his actions as a psycho-analyst are acts (as opposed to "acting out") and are expressions of a capacity for compassion. But a capacity for compassion is a source of admiration and therefore envy in an analysand who feels incapable of mature compassion.

It follows that it is a matter of difficulty for the analyst to conduct himself in such a manner that his association with the analysand is beneficial to the analysand. The exercise, in the patient's view, is the establishment of the superiority of rivalry, envy and hate over compassion, complementation and generosity. The crux to which I referred is found in the character of the co-operation between two people and not in the problem for which the co-operation is required. The nature of the co-operation may be determined by the disturbances in the personality of the patient, but that situation may be presumed to be amenable to psycho-analysis; it differs from the situation produced by the inborn disposition of the patient. If analysis has been successful in restoring the personality of the patient he will approximate to being the person he was when his development became compromised. His disturbed state may be the outcome of an inadequate solution of his problem, but when that situation has been psycho-analytically reconstructed the need arises to solve the problem more adequately. If rivalry, envy and hate are secondary the chance of an adequate solution would seem to be greater than would be the case if the patient's endowment of rivalry, envy and hate is intrinsic, inborn, the very stuff of his personality.

The more the problem relates to the patient's inborn character the more difficult it is for him to modify his adherence to transformation in hallucinosis as *the* superior approach. If his solution were determined by a false belief that no real solution exists it would be easier for him to admit his mistake than it is when his solution is dictated by an inborn need to be "top". This would be unimportant were it not for the belief that certain disorders, notably schizophrenia, are physical and originate in pathological physical states. Their nature would be easier to grasp if seen to originate in a *normal* physical state and to spring from the very health and virility of the patient's endowment of ambition, intolerance of frustration, envy, aggression and his belief that there is, or ought to be, or will be (even if it has to be created by himself) an ideal object that exists to fulfil itself. The impression such patients give of suffering from a character disorder derives from the sense that their well-being and vitality spring from the same characteristics which give trouble. The sense that loss of the bad parts of his personality is inseparable from loss of that part in which all his mental health resides, contributes to the acuity of the patient's fears. This acute fear is inseparable from any attempt to resolve the crux. Is the patient going to repeat the former error by becoming confirmed in his adherence to transformation in hallucinosis or will he turn to transformation in psycho-analysis?

The generally accepted view amongst psycho-analysts is that interpretations are expressed verbally, that they should be terse and to the point, namely to make the patient aware of his unconscious motivations. The orthodox view can be expressed in my terms thus: the medium of transformation is conversational English. The analyst's statements should belong to categories F_1, 3, 4. The link with analysand should be K, not H or L. He should not express himself in any terms other than those used by an adult; theoretically this excludes certain categories (notably column 2) but, as I have shown, it is possible to regard the patient's statement in different ways, so that sometimes one dimension is thrown into relief, at other times another, and it is equally open to the patient to do just that. It is because he does so that his response to an interpretation may appear anomalous. Therefore although the analyst is under an obligation to speak with as little ambiguity as possible, in fact his aims are limited by the analysand who is free to receive interpretations in whatever way he chooses. In a sense it can seem that the analyst is hoist with his own petard: he is free to interpret the statements of the analysand how he will; the analysand retorts in kind. The analyst is not free except in the sense that when the patient comes to him for analysis he is obliged to speak in a way which would not be tolerable in any other frame of reference and then only from a particular vertex.

The patient's response would also be intolerable if there were no psycho-analytic indulgence to excuse it, or, if it were not for a psycho-analytic vertex.

If the reader will reconsider the last page he will see a number of statements whose relationship to each other, and therefore meaning, is illuminated if we employ the concept of vertex thus:

"The generally accepted view amongst psycho-analysts . . ."—vertex 1

"The orthodox view . . ."—vertex 2

"Terms used by an adult . . ."—vertex 3

". . . analyst under an obligation . . ."—vertex 4 (implied, not stated)

". . . free to receive . . . he chooses . . ."—vertex 5 (receptor vertex)

". . . in a sense it can be seen . . ."—vertex 6

". . . the analyst . . . is obliged . . ."—vertex 7

". . . not be tolerable . . . in any other frame of reference . . ."—vertex 8.

All these vertices represent views with which I am identified. With myself as the vertex all these vertices represent "other-people-as-seen-by-me." Any view with which I am identified is, as I explained discussing O, a vertex from which I have separated myself or with which I have attempted to become-at-one; the direction of the link is immaterial in this context. "Other-people-as-seen-by-me" are phenomena. I can know phenomena: I can know various aspects of my personality with which I am identified. I can identify myself with aspects of myself which I can know. Any such identification or knowledge is formulated and thereby becomes a statement and, like every other statement in whatever medium, can be classified in a grid category. It is a transformation $T x\beta$. ($x =$ the personality in whom $T x\alpha$ has taken place.)

CHAPTER ELEVEN

In none of this have I spoken of O except in so far as the horizontal axis of the grid implies the existence of an object that "uses" and the vertical axis implies the existence of an object that "possesses" something to use.

My theory would seem to imply a gap between phenomena and the thing-in-itself and all that I have said is not incompatible with Plato, Kant, Berkeley, Freud and Klein, to name a few, who show the extent to which they believe that a curtain of illusion separates us from reality. Some consciously believe the curtain of illusion to be a protection against truth which is essential to the survival of humanity; the remainder of us believe it unconsciously but no less tenaciously for that. Even those who consider such a view mistaken and truth essential consider that the gap cannot be bridged because the nature of the human being precludes knowledge of anything beyond phenomena save conjecture. From this conviction of the inaccessibility of absolute reality the mystics must be exempted. Their inability to express themselves through the medium of ordinary language, art or music is related to the fact that all such methods of communication are transformations and transformations deal with phenomena and are dealt with by being known, loved or hated—K, L or H. Transformation then is intermediate between O and $T\,x\beta$. We must therefore consider further the gap between O and knowledge of phenomena and transformations of O.

The gap between reality and the personality, or, as I prefer to call it, the inaccessibility of O, is an aspect of life with which analysts are familiar under the guise of resistance. Resistance is only manifest when the threat is contact with what is believed to be real. There is no resistance to anything because it is believed to be false. Resistance operates because it is feared that the reality of the object is imminent. O represents this dimension of anything whatever—its reality.

It is not knowledge of reality that is at stake, nor yet the human equipment for knowing. The belief that reality is or could be known is mistaken because reality is not something which lends itself to being known. It is impossible to know reality for the same reason that makes it impossible to sing potatoes; they may be grown, or pulled, or eaten, but not sung. Reality has to be "been": there should be a transitive verb "to be" expressly for use with the term "reality".

When, as psycho-analysts, we are concerned with the reality of the personality there is more at stake than an exhortation to "know thyself, accept thyself, be thyself", because implicit in psycho-analytic procedure is the idea that this exhortation cannot be put into practice without the psycho-analytic experience. The point at issue is how to pass from "knowing" "phenomena" to "being" that which is "real".

To recapitulate: It is possible through phenomena to be reminded of the "form". It is possible through "incarnation" to be united with a part, the incarnate part, of the Godhead. It is possible through hyperbole for the individual to deal with the real individual. Is it possible through psycho-analytic interpretation to effect a transition from knowing the phenomena of the real self to being the real self?

If I am right in suggesting that phenomena are known but reality is "become" the interpretation must do more than increase knowledge. It can be argued that this is not a matter for the analyst and that he can only increase knowledge; that the further steps required to bridge the gap must come from the analysand; or from a particular part of the analysand, namely his "godhead", which must consent to incarnation in the person of the analysand.

Here there seems to be a matter of "direction": it is not the same for the "godhead" to consent to incarnation in the person of the analysand as for the analysand to consent to "becoming" god or the "godhead" of which "god" is the phenomenological counterpart. The latter, at any rate, would seem to be closer to insanity than mental health.

The problem, psycho-analytically, is easier to grasp if O

represents ultimate reality, good and evil. Becoming O would then seem to be easier to associate with cure than becoming ultimate good or ultimate evil by splitting. Moreover, health may be more easily associated with being passive, *vis-à-vis* ultimate good and evil, rather than with being active.

The gap between "knowing phenomena" and "being reality" resembles the gap between "Knowing about psycho-analysis" and "Being psycho-analysed". The transition from "knowing phenomena" to "being reality" would seem certain to involve experience of modifying adherence to column 2 statements. It would appear to involve abandonment of making statements known to be false to form a barrier against statements believed to be true. If so, further consideration of column 2 categories offers a promising approach. In terms of resistance theory the aim of resistance is to preserve unconsciousness of thoughts, feelings and "facts", presumably because that is felt to be the best method, *in the circumstances*, of dealing with the problem presented by those thoughts, feelings and "facts". Resistance cannot however be evoked unless there is in operation the contrary feeling that consciousness is the best approach. A widely inclusive example of such conflict is provided by the personality who feels unable to improve defects whose existence he suspects and resorts to being unaware of what he feels unable to change. There are occasions in the life of everyone when it is felt to be wise, not pathological, to turn a "blind eye". Such situations become pathological when the "cure" achieved by these means is felt to be more painful that the original dis-ease. It is not always a matter of finding the "cure" more painful: if the exclusion of unwelcome elements is effected with a view to keeping thoughts relevant to the problem and free from distraction, then dissatisfaction is felt because the result of the exclusion is to prejudice the usefulness of the train of thought. In analysis the problem is not necessarily associated with any particular instance of column 2 operation but is associated with the habit of mind that resorts to column 2 mechanisms with such frequency that the state of "being" O is indefinitely postponed.

The first requisite is to detect the column 2 dimension of the statements that are being made. It may not be a significant dimension and in that case the analyst must use his judgment to decide what statement or statements he is going to treat in this way. In transforming the patient's statement he is ignoring its other dimensions just as, in the model with which I start this chapter, the rule for forming the second tray of marbles ignores all dimensions save the green glass of the marbles on the first tray; all dimensions except for one very important one—the *number* of green glass marbles. To this important exception I shall now turn.

Mathematicians are aware that the progress of arithmetic is obstructed probably through some unsolved problem with regard to the nature of the discipline. Psycho-analytically the problem can be approached in the manner I have laid down in this book. "Numbers" such as "many", "three", "one", "too much" are attempts to bind a constant conjunction, preparatory to understanding the conjunction. Numbers are signs denoting a constant conjunction and are an attempt to bind the constant conjunction, but the constant conjunction is itself a constant conjunction—a group of elements that are felt to be constantly conjoined. Number is an attempt to seize upon a system, so to speak, of a group and by naming it take the first step towards understanding, or finding a meaning for, the group. One, true to the negative quality of the definitory hypothesis (col. 1) is a denial of the group. All other numbers are likewise attempts, first to bind, then to understand, the group. It is an over-simplification to describe the object as a group: it is perhaps too mathematical to call it infinity, too mystical to call it the infinite, too religious to call it the Godhead.

Psychologically the problem commences with the impingement on the individual of an object containing in itself the potentiality of all distinctions as yet undeveloped, a group, a conjunction and the need to bind the "groupishness" of the group by a name, a column 1 element. If the initiative is felt to lie with the object its "distinctions" develop till such point as a "distinction" impinges on the individual; in so far as it is felt to lie with the individual his awareness develops to a point where some "distinction", or dimension as I have called it, appears to him to demand binding.

Verbal expressions intended to represent the ultimate object often appear to be contradictory within themselves, but there is a surprising degree of agreement, despite differences of background, time and space, in the descriptions offered by mystics who feel they have experienced the ultimate reality. Sometimes the agreement seems close even when, as with Milton, the individual seems to know of it rather than to have experienced it.

"The rising world of waters dark and deep
Won from the void and formless infinite."[1]

I am not interpreting what Milton says but using it to represent O. The process of binding is a part of the procedure by which something is "won from the void and formless infinite"; it is K and must be distinguished from the process by which O is "become". The sense of inside and outside, internal and external objects, introjection and projection, container and contained, all are associated with K.

Distinction between the "geometric" and "arithmetic" developments can be made thus: the geometric developments of points and line are primarily associated with the presence or absence, existence or non-existence, of an object. The arithmetic development is associated with the state of the object, whether it is whole or fragmented, whole object or part object.

The geometric development is associated with depression, absence or presence of the object: the arithmetic development with feelings of persecution, the Kleinian theory of a paranoid-schizoid position.

When the dimensions of a statement are the presenting feature in analysis it is a matter of importance to observe whether the object is considered to have dimensions as a part of synthesis (K) or because the dimensions are seen as fragments unrelated to each other, the debris, as it were, of a splitting process (H).

[1] Milton, J.: *Paradise Lost*, Bk. III.

It may at first seem strange to suggest that groups or the infinite should be regarded as epistemologically prior to all else, but less so if we consider that only when a problem is intractable, or seems to be so, will it be felt to engage, and demand, our most powerful efforts. Reciprocally the more we feel ourselves deeply engaged the more likely we are to suppose that the problem *must* be intractable and that it is so intrinsically.

We may now reconsider some of the problems associated with ideas of causation. $T \beta$ is a formulated transformation, whatever the medium in which the transformation is expressed. $T \alpha$ is the process, employing α-elements, by which the individual arrives at $T \beta$. In thinking about transformation we may arrest the process, at whatever point we wish, to give ourselves the conditions in which to make our inspection. If carried to extremes the process of arrest can amount to a denial of the passage of time as in the instances I have cited of the disturbed state where time itself is destroyed by being reduced to a point and then denied altogether. Ignoring this extreme, but taking advantage of the freedom conferred by thought we may interrupt what in fact is a continuous process by inspecting $T \alpha$, $T \beta$ or O in as far as it can be possible to know, or be curious, *about* O. We can only have a K link with *transformations* of O. One dimension of O is expressed by terms such as "cause", or a "first cause".

The "cause" O may be felt to be present or absent, single or multiple, independent of the personality or hallucinated. O, in its "caused" dimension, as in all others, may be located in the Platonic Form, of which people and things are "reminders"; in a deity, of which people and things are "incarnations"; in hyperbole, of which people and things are containers. "Causation", as a dimension of O, has the characteristics of all other dimensions of O that are subjected to the various processes of transformation and inspected at various stages in the process.

Any statement should be assessed according to its grid category, re-assessed as $T \beta$ in accordance with its position in the Reality scale, that is Form and reminder, deity and incarnation, hyperbole and evacuation. The interpretation should be such that the transition from *knowing about* reality to *becoming real* is furthered. This transition depends on matching the analysand's statement with an interpretation which is such that the circular argument remains circular but has an adequate diameter. If it is too small the circular argument becomes a point; if too great it becomes a straight line. The point and straight line together with numbers are representatives of states of mind which are primitive and unassociated with mature experience. The profitable circular argument depends on a sufficiency of experience to provide an orbit in which to circulate. To re-state this in terms of greater sophistication, the analytic experience must consist of knowing and being successively many elementary statements, discerning their orbital or circular or spherical relationship and establishing the statements which are complementary. The interpretations that effect the transition from knowing about O to becoming O are those establishing complementarity: all others are concerned with establishing the material through which the argument circulates.

The transition from "knowing about" to "becoming" O can be seen as a particular instance of the development of the conception from the pre-conception (row E from row D). I have described that process as one of saturation of an unsaturated element $\psi(\xi)$, to become $\psi(\psi)(\xi)$. That is to say, a pre-conception becomes a conception and retains its dimension of "usability" as a pre-conception. The transition, in terms of transformation, may be formulated as $T\alpha \rightarrow T\beta$ (cycle 1), $T\beta$ (cycle 1) $\rightarrow T\alpha$ (cycle 2). The psycho-analytic conception of cure should include the idea of a transformation whereby an element is saturated and thereby made ready for further saturation. Yet a distinction must be made between this dimension of "cure" or "growth" and greed. To this I shall revert after considering "arithmetic" further. I should say, if it is not already clear, that the domain of mathematics with which I am concerned is the "Dodgsonian" or "Alice Through the Looking-Glass" variety.

I have said numbers are a means of binding (col. 1) a constant conjunction. By definition this means that the conjunction is unknown or devoid of meaning. O is not known, but for ease in exposition I am supposing that the conjunction, or part of a conjunction, which is to be bound with a view to investigation, is the "group". The number signified by 1 is a way of denoting a whole object which is not a group. The group is infinite, whether it is a group of people, things or "causes". From this we may proceed to emotional mathematics (or the mathematics of emotion) thus: $1 =$ "one is one and all alone and evermore shall be so". $\frac{1}{1} =$ a relationship with "the whole of an object that is a whole object, that is unrelated to any other objects and therefore has no properties; since properties are a dimension of relationships." With religion as vertex this sign can represent the O represented by the term "Godhead". With a Miltonic vertex it is represented by the "void and formless infinite" from which is "won" the object that is known. With a Dantesque vertex it is represented by the 33rd canto of the Paradise. With a mathematical vertex, and regarding it in its negative aspect of definition, it can be represented by the term "not infinity".

Similarly $\frac{1}{2}$ can represent, in its column 1 dimension, a relationship with a part of a part of a group. In its negative dimension it denies that there are more than, or less than, two in the group and affirms that the relationship is with one of them.

When formulated these numbers can be used in the process of transformation. They can be combined with other numbers as and when other numbers are formulated. The development is therefore two-fold: the group can be denoted by a new number whenever a constant conjunction is felt to require binding, as for example if a number "two" is felt to be necessary because O is not felt to be represented by 1. Thus development can proceed according to a plan of enumeration. Or, curiosity about the relationship of 1 to $\frac{1}{1}$ or $\frac{1}{2}$ to O, and from that to the relationship that each has to the other, leads to manipulation and combination of the numbers. A religious counterpart can be seen in St Augustine's formulation in *The City of God* that only when the individual has regulated his relationship with God (O, or more precisely 1, for the relationship with God is possible, but not with the Godhead because the latter is Darkness and Formlessness, potentially containing all distinctions but yet undeveloped), can he regulate his relationship with his fellow men.

The combination and manipulation of numbers is stimulated by the same force as stimulates their formulation—the awareness of a constant conjunction that requires to be bound.

Manipulation and combination of numbers lead to mathematical formulation as it is ordinarily understood; these formulations (or formulae) may be regarded as D category and used as elements in column 3 and 4 categories are used (or, of course, as elements in any other columns are used). In their category 3 and 4 dimensions they may then be used in the exploration of the world as it is ordinarily supposed by scientists to exist. The spur to the investigation is still the same spur that led to the binding of the constant conjunctions in the first instance. The domain investigated, whether it be called Platonic memories, or religious incarnations, or hyperbole (in the sense in which I have used the term) containers and contained, supplies further stimulation in that each D3 and D4 statement requires further saturation. Evidently the impulse to achieve saturation is unlikely to be fulfilled because in addition to the limitations of human capacity there is the factor of "the void and formless infinite" which, whether thought of as in the mind of man or outside it, cannot be known but must be "become," that is, saturated in a particular way.

Psycho-analysts may find what I have said about theories of causation in the context of Transformation, as it exists in *knowing about* and *becoming* O, more familiar if they remember how big a part is played in analysis by the need to blame other people and the difficulties of maturation because maturation involves *being* responsible.

The function of T α is to lead to T β, which in turn must lead to growth, and therefore must be capable of categorization in D3 or D4. In K, a domain in which it is sufficient to know *about* something, the apparatus of pre-conception and transformation leads to repetition but in a new cycle. We need to know what kind of transformation (T$\alpha \to$ Tβ) is required to effect the transition from K to "becoming" or "being". The discovery of the Differential Calculus by Gallileo, Newton and Descartes produced a weapon adequate to deal with K phenomena in their inanimate dimension. But it does not produce growth, only permits accretions of knowledge about growth. The differential calculus may be described as D3 and D4 category in K and must therefore be seen as an instrument furthering K, but not O. It is *conducive* to becoming, or being O, but has nothing to say about its place in that transformation. We do not learn from it what part it plays, or what the process is in which it plays a part, by which T $\alpha \to$ T $\beta =$ K $\to$ O.

To rigid motion transformations, projective transformations, transformations in hallucinosis, I shall now add transformations in O. That is to say I propose to extend the significance O to cover the domain of reality and "becoming". Transformations in O contrast with other transformations in that the former are related to growth in becoming and the latter to growth in "knowing about" growth; they resemble each other in that "growth" is common to both.

Transformation in K has, contrary to the common view, been less adequately expressed by mathematical formulation than by religious formulations. Both are defective when required to express growth, and therefore transformation, in O. Even so, religious formulations come nearer to meeting the requirements of transformations in O than mathematical formulations. I shall illustrate my meaning by discussing first, Berkeley's objection to Halley and Newton's formulation in his "Opticks of the Differential Calculus", which Halley sponsored, and second, the phenomenon known to analysts as Resistance.

CHAPTER TWELVE

BISHOP BERKELEY, prompted by the irreligion of Newton and his sponsor Edmund Halley, attacked certain illogicalities, notably circular argument, in Newton's presentation of the differential calculus; his criticisms exercised mathematicians for over a century. The following quotation is from *The Analyst* (published in 1734):

"It must, indeed, be acknowledged that he used fluxions, like the scaffold of a building, as things to be laid aside or got rid of as soon as finite lines were found proportional to them. But then these finite exponents are found by the help of fluxions. Whatever therefore is got by such exponents and proportions is to be ascribed to fluxions: which must therefore be previously understood. And what are these fluxions? The velocities of evanescent increments. And what are these same evanescent increments? They are neither finite quantities, nor quantities infinitely small, nor yet nothing. May we not call them the ghosts of departed quantities?"

Newton's formulation of the differential calculus is a transformation in K. "The ghosts of departed quantities" expresses the negative of the column 1 dimension of his formulation. The transformation in K is effected by discarding the "scaffolding" of fluxions, "the ghosts of departed quantities". The discarding of the scaffolding may be regarded as a step to achieve finite lines "proportional to them", a category H3 formulation; or, "the finite lines . . . proportional to them" may be regarded as an F3 formulation used as a column 2 formulation to prevent emergence of the "ghosts of departed quantities" and the psychological turbulence that such an emergence would precipitate; Newton did have what we would today regard as a psychotic breakdown in which, in his own words, he lost "the former consistency of his mind" and from which he emerged, according to J. M. Keynes, "slightly 'gaga'". Keynes's paper, which was read by his brother at the Centenary Celebrations held in July 1946, contains material which will repay study for its penetrating insights though I cannot enter into it here.

Berkeley's formulation may be regarded as an F3 contribution. The polemical tone gives it a column 2 category, denying, though he acknowledges the truth of Newton's result, the validity of the method: the ironic tone denies the reality of "the ghosts of departed quantities". The pamphlet as a whole is thus an example of an F3 formulation used, in its second cycle, as column 2 to deny both the "ghosts" component and the H3 component in his and Newton's confrontation. From a psycho-analytic vertex both formulations, Newton's and Berkeley's, can be seen as $T \beta$ col. 3 (intended to produce a formulation $T \beta$ (col. 3) (cycle 2)), or, $T \beta$ col. 2 (intended to deny emergence of β-elements).

T Newton β H3 furthers mathematic inquiry: T Newton β col. 2 denies the "ghosts". T Berkeley β col. 2 denies, by irony, "ghosts" and, by polemic, the scientific approach. In both instances the col. 2 dimension is directed against psychological turbulence; why? for fear of the turbulence and its associated "becoming". Put in other terms, transformations in K are feared when they threaten the emergence of transformations in O. This can be restated as fear when $T\alpha \rightarrow T\beta = K \rightarrow O$. Resistance to an interpretation is resistance against change from K to O. Change from K to O is a special case of Transformation; it is of particular concern to the analyst in his function of aiding maturation of the personalities of his patients.

My term "psychological turbulence" needs elucidation. By it I mean a state of mind the painful quality of which may be expressed in terms borrowed from St John of the Cross. I quote:[1]

> "The first (night of the soul) has to do with the point from which the soul goes forth, for it has gradually to deprive itself of desire for all the worldly things which it possessed, by denying them to itself; the which denial and

---

[1] *The Ascent of Mount Carmel*, 1, 1 and 2.

deprivation are, as it were, night to all the senses of man. The second reason has to do with the mean, or the road along which the soul must travel to this union—that is, faith, which is likewise as dark as night to the understanding. The third has to do with the point to which it travels—namely, God, Who, equally, is dark night to the soul in this life."

I use these formulations to express, in exaggerated form, the pain which is involved in achieving the state of naivety inseparable from binding or definition (col. 1). Any naming of a constant conjunction involves admission of the negative dimension and is opposed by the fear of ignorance. Therefore at the outset there is a tendency to precocious advance, that is, to a formulation which is a col. 2 formulation intended to deny ignorance—the dark night of the senses. The relevance of this to psychological phenomena springs from the fact that they are not amenable to apprehension by the senses; this tends to precipitate transformation into such objects as *are* and so contributes to Transformation in hypochondriasis. The "col. 1" elements thus formed are liable to be second cycle col. 2—transformations which are $T \beta$ col. 1 → $T \beta$ (second cycle) col. 2.

Similarly the intuitive approach is obstructed because the "faith" involved is associated with absence of inquiry, or "dark night" to K.

The third "dark night" is associated with the transformation in O, that is from $K \rightarrow O$. The transformation that involves "becoming" is felt as inseparable from becoming God, ultimate reality, the First Cause. The "dark night" pain is fear of megalomania. This fear inhibits acceptance of being responsible, that is mature, because it appears to involve *being* God, being the First Cause, being ultimate reality with a pain that can be, though inadequately, expressed by "megalomania".

The same tensions are involved in all transformations in O and these I shall now discuss.

Interpretations are part of K. The anxiety lest transformation in K leads to transformations in O is responsible for the

form of resistance in which interpretations appear to be
accepted but in fact the acceptance is with the intention of
"knowing about" rather than "becoming". In other terms,
it is an acceptance to preserve the K link as a col. 2 element
against transformation in O. By agreeing with the interpretation it is hoped that the analyst will be inveigled into a
collusive relationship to preserve K without being aware
that he is doing so. If the manoeuvre is successful transformations in K fulfil an F_2 role preventing the inception of
$T\alpha \rightarrow T\beta = K \rightarrow O$.

For the next step in this discussion I shall regard the
Kleinian theory of Projective Identification as a psycho-
analytic formulation (row F categories) based on a background of realizations encountered in analytic practice and
in every-day life: these realizations I shall name "hyperbole". "Hyperbole" is a term belonging to the system of
Theories of Observation in contrast to the theory of
Projective Identification which I regard as a term belonging
to the system of Psycho-Analytical Theory. I do not propose
to discuss the system of Psycho-Analytical Theory. For that
I refer the reader to the work of Bowlby and the Research
Committee of the British Psycho-Analytical Society of which
he is Chairman, Sandler and his co-workers, Segal and her
introduction to Melanie Klein and Wisdom on the theories
of Klein and Fairbairn. The domains of Theories of
Observation and Theories of Psycho-Analysis overlap but
the problem is simplified if a distinction is made and can be
preserved. The workers on the Theories of Psycho-Analysis,
to whom I have referred, are engaged on a task which
should lead to precise determination and formulation of
psycho-analytic theory and eventually to a corpus which
belongs uniformly to the category row F. "Hyperbole" is
the term I give, in theories of observation, to the realizations
that correspond to the theory of projective identification.

The following is a series of statements used as illustrations:

1. I have always believed you are a very good analyst.
2. I knew a woman in Peru, when I was a child, who had
   second sight.

3. It seems to me psycho-analysts would do better if they believed in God: God *can* cure.

4. There ought not to be so much pain and suffering in the world. What can a mere human being do?

The interpretation of these statements would depend on circumstances which I cannot report here; the suggestions I make must be seen as related to exposition and not clinical experience.

Comment:

1. (*a*) The goodness of the analyst stops short, as it were, in my person. I am "it".

(*b*) The goodness of the analyst is incarnate in me. I am the embodiment of analytic goodness.

(*c*) The goodness of the analyst is incorporated in me. Either I have obtained possession of the goodness of the analyst by "taking it into" myself or some force has "put it into" me.

Which of these statements represents the facts most closely depends on the judgment the analyst forms in the emotional experience itself.

2. (*a*) The goodness of the analyst has been projected a long way in time and place. This is hyperbole; there is something in the experience with the analysand that makes this term suitable for binding the particular conjunction, and none other (the negative dimension of the definition), which I want to examine. The term already marks a conjunction (the positive dimension of the definitory hypothesis) which is present in the conjunction to which I want to draw attention, namely the early meaning of hyperbole as a "throwing beyond" someone else, signifying rivalry.

(*b*) The goodness of the analyst has been thrown "into" the woman, or Peru, or the past.

The analyst will have to decide according to the experience what further qualities are conjoined with the qualities represented by the term "hyperbole". For example, is the goodness incarnate in the woman or incorporated by her, or projected into her, and if so by whom? And who or where is the rival?

These questions, often answered implicitly, require a

means for making them explicit; this is aided by the grid and the Theory of Transformations. The term "hyperbole" has a history which fits it for compact representation of a number of clinical statements which (i) occur frequently, (ii) are easily recognizable as instances of hyperbole and (iii) are almost certainly symptomatic of a constant conjunction which has significance for the personality being analysed and for the main body of psycho-analytic theories of idealization, splitting, projective identification, rivalry and envy. In grid categorical terms it can be classified as row A (β-elements), row C (the visual or pictorial dimension), row D and row E. It has therefore a wide spectrum, is flexible and lends itself easily for use by the analyst as a "selected fact" to aid in displaying coherence which, without it, may not be apparent. "Hyperbole" can be regarded as representing hyperbole and hyperbole is projection conjoined with rivalry, ambition, vigour which can amount to violence and hence to "distance" to which an object is projected. By "distance" I mean something which is the "ghost of a departed quantity" or, to put it in another way, distance $= \psi(\xi)$ where $(\xi) =$ a non-existent quantity. It could be where quantity was or where it will be but not where it *is*; it represents an unsaturated element, an evanescent increment or "departed quantity". I shall reconsider O with the help of (ξ), Platonic Forms and their "reminders" (phenomena); "godhead", "god" and "his" incarnations; Ultimate Reality or Truth and the phenomena which are all that human beings can know of the thing-in-itself: all three possess a similar configuration. Milton can invoke light which at the voice of God invested

> "The rising world of waters dark and deep
> Won from the void and formless infinite."

Eckhart considers Godhead to contain all distinctions as yet undeveloped and to be Darkness and Formlessness. It cannot be the object of Knowledge until there flows out from it Trinity and the Trinity *can* be known. According to Kant the thing-in-itself cannot be known but secondary and primary qualities can be. Examples of similar configurations can be multiplied but for my purposes these are sufficient to indicate, without I hope distorting the historical meanings that the authors wished to formulate, what I mean to signify by O. According to need it may be supposed that (i) from O undeveloped distinctions evolve, or, that (ii) from O, the "void and formless infinite", the individual (sense) and group (common sense) win secondary and primary qualities (in Kant's sense). The "winning" of qualities is part of K. In so far as potentialities and distinctions "evolve" from O it is a part of becoming or Transformation in O. Transformations in K may be described loosely as akin to "knowing about" something whereas Transformations in O are related to becoming or being O or to being "become" by O. The "distance" (ξ) between O and T β may be artificially described in a series of stages. Assuming a direction O $\rightarrow$ Tβ, O can be said to "evolve" by (a) becoming manifest (or "knowable") Tβ K $\rightarrow$ (b) by becoming a "reminder", an "incarnation" or "embodiment" or an "incorporation". $\rightarrow$ (c) by becoming Tβ O or, "at-one-ment". Assuming the reverse direction Tβ $\rightarrow$ O, the individual proceeds (Tα K) $\rightarrow$ (a) Tβ K, (col. 1) definition, $\rightarrow$ (b) Tβ K (cycle 1) = Tα K (cycle 2) $\rightarrow$ Tβ K (cycle 2) (col. 3) memory or notation "reminder", "incarnation", or "incorporation" $\rightarrow$ (c) Tβ (cycle n $-$ 1) = Tα K (cycle n) $\rightarrow$ Tβ O.

As I have said resistances, though apparently K phenomena, derive from Transformations in O. Hatred and fear derive from the fact that transformations in K threaten the further transformation represented by T β (cycle n $-$ 2) $\rightarrow$ T β (cycle n $-$ 1) = T α (cycle n) K $\rightarrow$ Tβ O.

The resistance based on hatred and fear of T K $\rightarrow$ T O manifests itself as preference for knowing about something to becoming something. The photograph representing Monet's Les Coquelicots (or any other artistic representation) is preferred to exposure to the painting itself: exposure to the painting is restricted to perceiving that it is "about" a field of poppies. No matter what the domain may be the resistance by "knowing about" against "becoming" is sure to be in evidence and is by no means restricted to psycho-analysis. Nevertheless in analysis, where analyst and patient must hope for growth in a capacity for maturation, this aspect of T K → T O is important and must be considered further. Any interpretation may be accepted in K but rejected in O; acceptance in O means that acceptance of an interpretation enabling the patient to "know" that part of himself to which attention has been drawn is felt to involve "being" or "becoming" that person. For many interpretations this price is paid. But some are felt to involve too high a price, notably those which the patient regards as involving him in "going mad" or committing murder of himself or someone else, or becoming "responsible" and therefore guilty. There is one class of interpretations, which seems to illuminate good qualities, to which the objection is not so easy to understand. The extreme example, interpretations which involve "becoming O" are dreaded as inseparable from megalomania, or what the psychiatrists or public might name delusions of grandeur or other diagnosis implying grave pathological disorder. The public or psychiatric view is more important than might appear as it introduces the social or group component in mental disorder and its treatment. To this I shall now turn.

A patient will manipulate his analysis and his environment in a manner which is consistent, determined, bearing the impress of a plan which is set but of which the pattern remains obscure. With most patients it is easy to understand that his disabilities are a trial to himself and his associates but with a few his pain, obvious enough, seems to matter far less to him than it does to everyone else, including the analyst. Relatives and associates are frightened by his irresponsibility into accepting, however powerless they may be, the responsibility he will not accept himself: he who has the power won't exercise it, they, who have not, are forced to do so. His company, so painful to himself, is nurtured and developed so that it will be even more painful to others. Granted the necessary endurance and a capacity to combine observation with it, certain characteristics begin to emerge; here are some:

1. Whenever the patient arouses pity or compassion he associates it with "statements" that leave the analyst a

choice between hating the patient or feeling that he has been guilty of inexperience of the world as it is.

2. Associated with 1. above the analysand exudes a sense of his superiority, an aloofness from humanity and the particular specimen that is his analyst. How he does this must be experienced in detail by the analyst and demonstrated to the analysand.

3. The patient's statements give an impression, sharp enough to evoke forebodings in the analyst yet vague enough to evoke forebodings about the forebodings. The qualities of 1. and 2. above are thus in evidence, "splitting" the analyst by leaving him evenly balanced on the horns of a dilemma, unable to remain indecisive and unable to decide on one interpretation without misgivings that the other was correct, thus contributing to the establishment of the superiority of the analysand. The additional feature is the forebodings. They derive from the patient's transformations, composed of category A3 and C3 elements, which are again transformed (cycle 2) into col. 6 elements for corrective purposes. The analyst finds himself in the following dilemma: the patient's statements (hints, clues, innuendos) give every reason to suppose that some grave threat to analyst and analysis is impending, the patient himself being all unaware of any cause for anxiety. These same statements are also made to carry an innuendo that if the analyst thinks the patient is "all unaware" of what is happening the analyst must be as inferior as the analysand thinks. If the analyst gives an interpretation the patient will make a new statement showing that he is unaware of what the analyst has said but that, according to the interpretation the analyst has given, either (*a*) the analyst is unaware of the feelings that all men of common sense would be bound to entertain about his conduct of the case, or, (*b*) the analyst is, without cause, feeling persecuted. The total experience, typical of many, demonstrates the crudity of expression and of the ideas expressed by the analyst as contrasted with the subtlety and evocative potency[1] of the analysand's ideas and methods of expression. Further the analysand has demonstrated the

[1] Cf. Bion, W. R.: *Learning from Experience*—beta-screen.

superiority of the aim to exacerbate pain over the aim to alleviate it.

From observation in the consulting-room the analyst is left to deduce the patient's skilful use of psychological insight in manipulation of the individual (the analyst) and the group (the patient's associates outside the consulting-room).

To sum up briefly: The theories of splitting, projective identification, persecution by the projected (evacuated) split-off elements have their approximate realization in the personality of the analysand. These realizations in the domain of the analysand's personality have been transformed (projective transformation), Tp β, the elements of which belong to row A (2nd cycle B $\leftrightarrow$ H) and col. 6 (second cycle 1, 2, 3, 4, 5, all $-$K). This transformation is then used in the consulting-room to destroy the analyst's psycho-analytic capacity and the psycho-analytic intercourse between analysand and analyst. To sum up in still more general terms, the analysis has been changed into a contest between (*a*) thought against action, (*b*) therapeutic use of insight against insight used to exacerbate, (*c*) pairing and dependent group against flight-fight group, (*d*) individual against group.

The patient's dilemma, in so far as he too is trying to be co-operative, reparative and creative, lies in his having to choose between "sanity" which is powerful, destructive and devoted to exacerbation, on the one hand, and creativeness which is impotent and "insane" on the other. If he wishes to be destructive his choice is between sanity which is creative and destructiveness which is insane. Strength of the desire is the determining factor. It has to be observed that this attempt at simplification by summary is vulnerable through its crudity. In the treatment of such cases there is no signification that is not over-simplification and no subtlety of discrimination that is not over-subtlety.

The complexity of a statement whether made by analyst of analysand imposes choice on the analyst; he must decide what dimension of the patient's statement he is to interpret and in what terms he will interpret it. To a great extent the choice is already determined by the analyst's personality and historical development and with those factors I do not intend to deal; I am concerned more with the immediate circumstances and those factors which are under the analyst's conscious control. He must beware of interpretation for no better reason than that the interpretation is one he can make. He cannot "win" it "from the void and formless infinite" of the analysand's personality, but only from the elements of the statement that the analysand has won from his own "void and formless infinite". Nothing is to be gained from telling the patient what he already knows unless what he "knows" is being used to exclude what he "is" (K opposed to O). Such an interpretation is part of the circular argument of which the "diameter" is too small: similarly the interpretation can be too abstruse and belong to a circular argument of which the "diameter" is too great. How is the "diameter" to be measured? If the interpretation is made mainly because it is available it is a col. 2 statement intended to prevent "turbulence" in the analyst. The abstruse interpretation relates to desire in the analyst, a wish to feel that he can see further than his analysand or some other who serves as a rival. It belongs to the domain of hyperbole. Too small and too large diameters indicate defence against and projection of hyperbole: defence is against hyperbole originated by the analysand.

Any statement may be supposed to include dimensions represented by every grid category. Not all dimensions have evolved (or been won) from the formlessness in which the potentiality for all distinctions exists. Therefore a statement can lack a varying number of classifiable dimensions because they remain undifferentiated potentialities. Epistemologically a statement may be regarded as evolved when any dimension can have a grid category assigned to it. For purposes of interpretation the statement is insufficiently evolved until its column 2 dimension is apparent. When the column 2 dimension has evolved, the statement can be said to be ripe for interpretation; its development as material for interpretation has reached maturity.

It is to be noted that a statement may be true in the context to which the analysand considers it to be relevant and yet have a column 2 dimension; it has a context to which its relevance is its column 2 dimension. A simple example of this is provided by statements which are recitals of common sense facts intended to deny expression to phantasy; the "fact" in this context is a theory known to be false.

A distinction must be made between the genesis of thought in the patient's life history and the genesis of expressions of thought in a given contingency. The emergence of the column 2 dimension may be observed in the contingency of the analysis as a step in the evolution of the statement and from it the analyst can judge that the conditions for interpretation have arrived; but it does not mean that an interpretation must be made; for the analyst's thought also must reach maturation. When he can see the column 2 element in his thoughts the conditions for interpretation are complete: an interpretation should be made. In terms of analytic theory it is approximately correct, but only approximately, to say that the conditions for an interpretation have arrived when the patient's statements provide evidence that resistance is operating: the conditions are complete when the analyst feels aware of resistance in himself—not countertransference which must be dealt with by analysis of the analyst, but resistance to the reaction he anticipates from the analysand if he gives the interpretation. Note the similarity of the analyst's resistance to the response he anticipates from the patient to his interpretation and the patient's resistance to the analyst's interpretation: the response anticipated by the analyst is coloured by his α-element version of the interpretation of his interpretation.

So far the "distance" between the analysand's statement (association) and the analyst's statement (interpretation) has been stated in terms of time required for the emergence of the column 2 element in the statement of the analysand and "proto-resistance", to coin a phrase, in the analyst to a response that has not yet been made. The analyst's proto-resistance must be projection of his own resistance to one dimension of his proposed interpretation. The interpretation he does give is a theory, known to be false, *vis-à-vis* an unknown contingent circumstance, but maintained as a barrier against turbulence expected to occur were it not so maintained; no statement is without a realization to which it stands in a col. 2 relationship. Thus a religious statement known to be false is used to exclude an aesthetic or scientific or other statement and vice versa.

In O the falsity of the statement is secondary to the fact that it is known to be so for it is the latter that inhibits growth whereas the former is part of human inadequacy. In K the fact that the statement is known to be false is secondary to the fact that it is so for it is the latter that inhibits the establishment of meaning whereas the former is part of individual maladjustment. Since the analyst is concerned with development of the personality it follows that the falsity of the statement will vary in significance according to its grid category and the transformation of which it is a part. To illustrate: suppose the statement is "the sun will rise tomorrow". If the patient is summarizing a weather forecast his statement is a form of notation or forecast. It is false because the sun does not rise but its employment is not to deny a fact but to explore possibilities. The category would be D3 or 4 according to the judgment of the person to whom the statement is made. If the statement has been made in analysis and is an expression of optimism it may be his transformation of feelings engendered by an interpretation he has just been given. If so it is transformation denoted by Tp β in O. But if he means he is going out with his girl friend its category is C3; it is an instance of hyperbole and the configuration of which it is a part is quite different from that of which the previous interpretation is a part. The words are the same, but the first example is D3 and 4 and the second C3. There is no intrinsic merit in establishing the category, but the attempt to do so forces clarification in the analyst's mind of what it is he is actually observing. For example: assuming the category to be C3 and that the girl *is* his friend it would follow that the link is L, the hyperbole an element in L (approximating to psycho-analytic theories of idealization) and the transformation a rigid motion transformation (approximating to psycho-analytic theories of transference).

Granting that the above is an adequate description of the analyst's transformation (Ta β) he may then enter on a second cycle of transformation in which the total statement is felt to be a denial of hostility. Ta β (cycle 1) then becomes Ta α (cycle 2). In the second cycle $= \text{Tp } \beta = \text{T } \alpha$ (cycle 2) $= \text{C}_3$ cycle 2 $= \text{D}_2$ and the statement, apparently loving idealization, is a denial of hostility to the analyst. The hyperbole is then a projection of the patient's hostility. This entirely alters the configuration, for the patient's transformation Tp β now appears to be a projective transformation, intended to rid himself of his hostility to the analyst, and approximates to the Kleinian theory of projective identification.

It is said that a discipline cannot properly be regarded as scientific until it has been mathematized and I may have given the impression, by adumbrating a Lewis Carol mathematics for analysis, that I support this view and in doing so risk the proposal of a premature mathematization of a subject which is not sufficiently mature for such a procedure. I shall therefore draw attention to some features of mathematical development which have not hitherto been adequately considered psycho-analytically. As an illustration I shall use the description, earlier in this chapter, of the transition from the dark and formless Godhead of Meister Eckhart to the "knowable" Trinity. My suggestion is that an intrinsic feature of the transition from the "unknow-ability" of infinite Godhead to the "knowable" Trinity is the introduction of the number "three". The Godhead has become, or been, mathematized. The configuration which can be recognized as common to all developmental processes whether religious, aesthetic, scientific or psycho-analytical is a progression from the "void and formless infinite" to a "saturated" formulation which is finite and associated with number, e.g. "three" or geometric, e.g. the triangle, point, line or circle. Associated with this is the need for a geometric or numerological component in effecting a transformation, e.g. in the model of the transformation of marbles on one tray to the marbles on the second tray. To what extent does this represent an essential link in the ability to effect transformations from experience of reality into knowledge of its manifestations from K to O? The transition from sensibility to awareness, of a kind suitable to be the foundation of action, cannot take place unless the process of change, T α, is mathematical though perhaps in a form that has not been recognized as such.[1]

I shall not discuss the topic here except in the resemblance of numeration to pre-conception (row D). It differs in that the problem seems to spring from a sense of "infinite" space, time, number which is then made finite. Confronted with the unknown, "the void and formless infinite", the personality of whatever age fills the void (saturates the element), provides a form (names and binds a constant conjunction) and gives boundaries to the infinite (number and position). Pascal's phrase "Le silence de ces espaces infines m'effraie" can serve as an expression of intolerance and fear of the "unknowable" and hence of the unconscious in the sense of the undiscovered or the unevolved.

The bearing on psycho-analysis and interpretation of what I have said may seem obscure; it is this: The beginning of a session has the configuration already formulated in the concept of the Godhead. From this there evolves a pattern and at the same time the analyst seeks to establish contact with the evolving pattern. This is subject to his Transformation and culminates in his interpretation Ta β. I am aware of the problems I have left without attempting an approach to their solution; some of these I hope to attempt later. In this book I draw attention to a few of the problems which present themselves in analytic material and offer suggestions for clarifying first, observation and then, assessment of what has been observed.

---

[1] A simple example of this is seen when an attempt is made to communicate, by means other than a full analysis, what a psycho-analysis is so that rules for its practice can be formulated: "five times" a week and for "50" minutes are readily "won" from the ineffable experience.

INDEX

Absence,
  of breast, as a place, 53
  used in accordance with grid 2,
    53
Acting-out,
  to be differentiated from acting,
    141
Action,
  and grid 6, 36
α-element,
  and dreams, before verbaliza-
    tion, 99
Aesthetic,
  experience, meaning as function
    of, 52
Agoraphobia
  and claustrophobia as fear of
    "space where something
    was", 123
Analyst,
  and change from patient's denial,
    14
  and cultural background, 10
  and psychotic transformation,
    6
  and realization, 4
  and supposed violence, 8
  and transformations of cata-
    strophe, 11
  "chronic" murder of, 28
  differences of transformation, 6
  experience of O, 24
  findings of, compared, 3
  his choice of interpretation, 26
  interpretations and transforma-
    tions, 5
  post- and pre-catastrophic in-
    variants, 9
  relatives' and analyst's anxieties,
    7
  sign for his transformations, 17
  state of mind in analysis, grid
    categories, 26
Analytic situation,
  as field onto which vertex is
    centrally projected, 112–13

Antidote,
  to problem preferred to its
    solution, 82
Aristotle,
  on definition and negation, 54,
    77
Art,
  contrasted with propaganda, 37
Attention,
  free-floating and wide spectrum
    of grid categories, 50

Babel,
  myth of confusion of language,
    58
Background,
  of cultural and analytic work, 10
β-element,
  confusion of metaphorical ex-
    pression in context of, 122
  mind operates on as if mind were
    a muscle, 130
  to take place of unsatisfactory
    descriptions, 78
  transformation from thought to
    action, 99
  use of concept of, 108
  vagueness of definition due to
    unfamiliarity of material,
    114
Berkeley. The Analyst
  criticism of Newton's fluxions,
    157
Bhāskara,
  comment on Theorem of Pytha-
    goras, 93
Biology,
  geometrical space corresponding
    to biological realization of
    emotion, 105
Bowlby, J.,
  research committee of *British
    Psycho-Analytical Society*, 160
Breast,
  absent, as place where breast
    was, 53